Family Camping Made Simple

Family Camping Made Simple

TENT AND RV CAMPING
WITH CHILDREN

by Beverly Liston

An East Woods Book

The Globe Pequot Press

Chester, Connecticut

Photograph on page 160 courtesy Howard Stone.

Library of Congress Cataloging-in-Publication Data

Liston, Beverly.
    Family Camping Made Simple: tent and RV camping with children/by
Beverly Liston. – 1st ed.
        p. cm.
    "An East Woods Book"
    Includes index.
    ISBN 0-87106-612-2
    1. Camping. 2. Family recreation. 3. Camping–equipment and sup-
plies. I Title.
GV191.7.L57 1989
796.54–dc20
                                                  89–7430
                                                    CIP

Manufactured in the United States of America
First Edition/First Printing

Contents

Preface

One morning some years ago, I woke up to fresh air, unfamiliar sounds, and a new lifestyle. I woke up to a day not only uncluttered by the usual duties and stresses but to a day that was "ours." It belonged to the family, and even the chores were going to be fun. We were not in a hurry to slither out of our sleeping bags. We worked together to build a fire and to prepare breakfast. By 10:00 A.M. the dishes were done, and the day was ours to plan and enjoy.

We had many activities to choose from—swimming, reading, having lunch by the lake, hiking, biking, driving to the nearby stables to take a guided ride, and more. We could think about barbecuing steak or hamburgers for dinner, try our luck at fishing for dinner, or cooking a stew all day in a special fire pit. Best of all, we felt a freedom in knowing that there was no problem with changing our minds along the way. Why? We were camping.

Later I saw the day growing dark and a fire blazing at our new home. While we sat around the fire—relaxed, reflecting, laughing, planning, and munching—I knew that we were all completely happy.

I took my first camping trip thirty years ago with my husband, Bob, and our baby daughter, Parmalee. I knew nothing about camping; my family had never gone on a camping trip or even a picnic. My husband was a beginner, too. On that first camping trip, we slept under the stars and ate from our picnic basket. Our daughter slept in a portacrib—the only piece of equipment we had.

We continued to camp, but out of necessity we began to focus on problem solving. We tangled with noodles that would not cook, with being cold at night, and with having inadequate equipment and a cramped car. We soon learned that the answers to all those problems lay in becoming acquainted with some basic camping information—the high-altitude cooking principle. the garment-layering principle, basic camping-gear facts, and car-packing tips.

We gradually improved our camping style as we increased our family to six children. We found a big canvas tent in good condition at a garage sale. We bought a propane stove at a flea market and began setting up special baskets of camp kitchen supplies. From then on every item was an exciting step to perfected camping. We got several ice chests, a dining canopy, a portable toilet, a utility trailer, and finally an inflatable boat. This was an exciting time of learning; we complimented ourselves on thinking of improvements—sometimes simple ones, like a fire starter for the propane stove, or something big, like a new tent that was much easier to put up.

Once we became more proficient campers, we were able to focus on the recreational aspect of our camping trips. We learned to plan at home and adopt a tentative schedule for every day (except arrival and departure, which we reserved for spontaneity). We looked into the opportunities of an area, sometimes calling in advance for specific information. Some of the attractions we enjoyed were a local drama festival and a scenic summer ride on a ski chairlift, along with sightseeing spots of all kinds, and new trails to hike. By purchasing an inflatable boat we could go to a new shore where we could sun, swim, or buy an ice-cream cone. Taking along our bicycles enabled us to travel to a special destination. Remembering to pack items such as a camera, wildflower identification guide, and binoculars gave us new hobbies to enjoy.

Camping trips soon became the highlight of the year for the children. With high anticipation they pitched in, eager to help. Their enthusiasm was a marvelous asset in family bonding. Bob and I were content watching them take so much pleasure in their camping activities. They dove off the pier at Sugar Pine Point at Lake Tahoe, they swam from rock to rock at Sand Harbor in Nevada, they read in a quiet spot on their beach towels, they floated around the lake on air mattresses, they took scenic pictures, and they never missed an evening campfire provided by the rangers.

Today, my family gets more excited than ever about a camping trip. There are four of us now in the core group (married children always welcome). My young daughters, Kyleen and Stephanie, now anticipate a guided horseback ride located near the campground—something we did not feature before. My husband and I never tire of our special walks. When we camp with our oldest daughter, her husband, and their children, we have gone full circle: Babies are once again at our campsite.

Given the choice, we would not select a vacation using motels, hotels, or guest-ranch facilities. They would not provide the ingredients that to us are so much fun. We love the overall free spirit and the simplicity that camping offers. We like setting up life on our own terms. We enjoy campsite housekeeping because it is simplified and different. We like opportunities for exercise that camping provides. And we appreciate being free of the restrictions that go along with the established home and community.

Remembering how awkward and insecure I felt as a beginning camper and realizing how we once had to use precious vacation time for learning made me realize the importance of writing a handbook for others. This book will help eliminate those first camping trips where everything goes wrong. My goal is to make the joys of camping available to all those families who would not have gone for lack of understanding the procedure from start to finish. If you want to know and experience the joy of camping, you will find out by reading this book. All the camping basics are here. Let me know how it goes; I'd like to hear about your trip. My mailing address is: P.O. Box 454, Los Altos, CA 94023-0454.

1

The Camping Experience

A 1986 Gallup poll ranked camping as the sixth most popular leisure activity among adults, and A. C. Neilsen reports that there are more than sixty million campers in the United States. Neither conclusion is surprising. Camping, after all, combines in a single activity what millions of people consider the prime ingredients of the "good life."

All too often today, people become enveloped in a technological cocoon and tend to think of life as a series of tasks and deadlines. Camping, however, erases these tensions of modern life; and once you return to simple patterns, you feel at peace. The simplicity and calm of the outdoors gives you the opportunity to think, react from within, and reflect. You can awaken in the morning to the sound of birds singing rather than the alarm clock ringing. You can dress comfortably and eat simple meals. You can live life on your own terms.

Camping allows a family to function as a unit and meet the needs of its individual members as well. Entire families plan a camping trip with excitement because there will be something for one and something for all. Individual differences can be reconciled in the wide range of activities that includes recreation, hobbies, flexible meal schedule, and housekeeping. At the same time the family can work together on mutual projects, reinforce the skills that cultivate family bonding, practice the give and take of cooperation, and renew the crucial art of listening. This cohesiveness will be a foundation for positive relationships long after the trip. Camping lets a family be a family.

Similarly, camping provides a wonderful way for meeting other people. Campers tend to form a camaraderie at campgrounds. They help each other with gear and starting cars; they chat about the environment and tourist attractions; they share food and matches. They meet people from all around the country and beyond, sometimes forming lasting friendships that are reinforced year after year at the same camping area.

Like no other vacation, camping offers endless opportunities for physical fitness. Setting up the campsite and maintaining the day's routine require physical activity. Camping chores are different from ordinary tasks done every day at home; the camper uses new muscles with fresh vigor, something you will notice when you set up your tent, chop a little wood, walk to the showers, and fetch your water.

When the tasks are done, the recreational opportunities involving physical fitness are endless. Hiking is one of the best activities for developing an invigorating physical pace. Scenic trails lead you through and to the grandeur of nature while you do your body a favor with some sensible exercise. Campgrounds often have bicycle paths. Bicycling can be moderate to strenuous. Just make some plans, take along a lunch, rest at scenic sites, and take some pictures. Campgrounds often are located near a lake or river, so canoeing and rowing are popular activities. Swimming at any hour of the day (try a swim just before breakfast or at bedtime!) is a luxury you come to take for granted.

Camping provides the beneficial counterpart to your routine pace. Those active at home can alter their pace with slow walks, sightseeing, sunning, and long naps in the hammock. Those who sit most of the day behind a desk can give their body a boost with long walks, swimming, and bike rides. That's the way with camping—it is tailored to fit one's needs.

Not to be overlooked is the enjoyment of nature that camping offers. You can learn to study the sky and recognize how different clouds and sky colors can indicate changes in the weather. You grow to appreciate the forces of nature—lightning, wind, temperature changes—and how they will affect you. Perhaps you learn to observe the ground squirrels and chipmunks around your campsite and see how they are similar but different, or maybe you get down on your hands and knees with your child to study a pill bug. At night you might go to a nearby lake and dangle a waterproof flashlight in the water to attract fish and observe them.

Living outdoors—camping—provides benefits both physical and mental. It fosters simplicity, companionship, physical fitness, relaxation, and an appreciation for the overwhelming details and majesty of nature. It is an experience anyone can have, regardless of age, income, background, and capabilities. Moreover, as the years go by, your camping skills will improve along with your knowledge of nature, your appreciation of family and new friends, your physical fitness, and your ability to slow down to a simpler life. Camping is a door to fulfillment. Open it.

2

Camping with Children

A camping trip with your children can be one of the most enjoyable family vacations you will ever take. Keep in mind, however, that it is wise to adjust the entire trip to the children's unique needs and capabilities. This approach will help you plan a trip that pleases everyone. High-speed sports, long automobile rides, and strenuous hikes need to be tailored when children are along. Focusing on children's interests and limitations can open up horizons that offer even more fun than a vacation without them.

Remember this axiom: Children will enjoy the camping vacation activities in proportion to their ability to respond positively to what is offered. Think about that. What is the key to their ability to respond? It is how they feel about themselves—in part, their physical and emotional satisfaction. Fortunately, vacation affords the time and the impetus to interact with one another in a way that provides physical and emotional satisfaction.

Within this climate of contentment is the freedom to enjoy to the fullest the activities involved in camping. Children can learn more than the facts. They absorb the whole picture that includes values about themselves, the activity, and you. For example, when you put up the hammock and use the opportunity to teach them the clove-hitch knot, unknowingly you also teach the value of relaxation, fun, and cooperation, and they will pick up on that.

Many of these activities are important to teach from the safety aspect alone. It is wise, for example, to explain the hazards of fuel when you demonstrate how to use the camp stove and lantern.

Do not overdo the teaching. There is a danger in overemphasizing what you want the child to learn—children can only absorb so much. The most important thing is that the children enjoy the vacation. They will be sensitive to your reaction about their rate of learning as well as their interest. Most important, they will learn about you as a teacher while you teach.

The following material should help you plan a successful camping trip, whatever your children's ages.

BABIES

Do not think that a baby cannot profit from the camping experience. The outdoor air, the rustling of nature, and the added family closeness are all appreciated by a baby. Enjoy including your baby in your camping activities—a dabble in the water, a little swing in the hammock, a ride on your back as you hike, a gaze at the stars (very bright and beautiful), and eye contact along with talk.

You probably will not be able to keep the baby on the same sleeping and eating schedule as at home, but do not worry about causing permanent damage to civilized habits. You can reestablish reasonable, scheduled living habits when you reach home.

Babies are not so fragile and frail as you are often led to believe. They will adjust to being in the woods. Simply apply your common sense, care, and parental love. For instance, you should be very careful about insects. Ask your pediatrician to recommend an insect repellent suitable for a baby's tender skin. If you would prefer not to put anything on the skin, you might try putting a little of the repellent on the baby's clothes. Protect the baby's skin from the sun. Use a sunscreen recommended for a baby, and keep his face shaded.

For a crawling infant, you need to be alert to the hazards in your new surroundings—the fire pit, a nearby stream, sticks, stones, and low-level strewn gear and personal items that are risky for a crawler.

Some extra attention needs to be given to packing for a baby on a camping trip.

Where will the baby sleep? If you are comfortable with letting the baby sleep with you in your sleeping bag, be certain to pack a piece of waterproof fabric sheeting to protect the sleeping bag. There also are many varieties of folding beds for infants, which would be nice to have on hand and would also serve as a clean, safe place for the baby to play. Mosquito netting or a tent screening fabric over the top and sides of the bed will help protect the baby from insects when napping outside the tent.

Other baby gear to consider are a sturdy infant seat that can be set on the ground (some of the infant-only car seats would be perfect here), a baby carrier (a backpack for a bigger infant and a carrier worn on your chest for a smaller infant), and a stroller. A carrier or a stroller is the ticket to including the baby on hikes and sightseeing. In buying a backpack, choose one that is comfortable on your back and

The stroller / carrier being used as chair

that the baby sits in securely. A good stroller for camping is one that positions flat for a naptime bed and has sturdy, smooth riding wheels to accommodate the rural terrain on trails. Other worthwhile features are sunshade, storage pockets, tray, and easy collapsing. The other advantage of a stroller is that it provides a place for the baby to be fed solid foods and stay clean, amused, and safe around the campsite.

If the baby is not nursing, plan to take plenty of formula and some plastic jugs of water from home. Water varies in different areas, and this change could be a problem for the baby.

When packing clothing, choose practical garments that will keep the baby warm and dry. It is a waste of time and added stress to be concerned about cute clothing. Since baby clothes do not take up much space, take an ample supply for all types of weather.

Consider the ecology issue if you generally opt for disposable diapers. Certainly there are dumpsters at established campgrounds, and you are permitted to use them for diapers. However, the disposable diapers do not decompose and are a menace to the soil. Campers are outdoor lovers. They learn to do what they can to protect the natural environment, which they enjoy so much. Read, talk, and think through this issue. Formulate your own family convictions. But when you backpack into areas where there are no garbage cans, the rule is: "Pack it in, pack it out." If you opt for cloth diapers, you will prefer the single layer ones because they will dry out quickly and even purify better than the prefolded diapers. Wash the diapers at least a hundred feet away from rivers, streams, or lakes. You do not need heavy soaped washings; do not be concerned about stains. Good rinsings with a little biodegradable soap and line or bush drying will be adequate. The important thing is to change wet and dirty diapers.

TODDLERS AND YOUNG CHILDREN

Toddlers and young children take naturally to the relaxation of the customary day-to-day standards on cleanliness and propriety. They will enjoy being outdoors and not being confined in a house where bric-a-brac and electric outlets are always "no-nos." This age likes the simple things that are in your new habitat: wildflowers, insects, chipmunks (but teach them not to pick the flowers or touch the animals).

The prime consideration for this age group is safety. Provide a confined place to keep your child when you are not steadily watching him. Consider taking along a playpen that doubles as a bed, a walker with removable wheels, a stroller with a tray for toys, a high chair or a table clamp-on seat, and/or a baby harness.

Since children this age tend to wander, pin a clanky bell to the back of their clothing, if the noise does not disturb others. Then there is no waiting until someone misses the child—you will know when your little explorer is leaving. This method works especially well with a toddler.

An additional precaution is to keep a name tag on each child. You can make a good name tag with a small, clear-plastic luggage tag on a lanyard. The information should include the child's name and age, important medical information, name of campground, number of your site, your vehicle make and license number, the name and phone number of a relative or close friend, and your doctor's name and phone number.

Campsite hazards for a baby also apply to children in this age group. In addition, be especially careful about the road around the campground. There are some typical campsite items that must be positioned with care for a young child's safety. Arrange pans on the camp stove with their handles pointed away from the child's reach. Keep hazardous kitchen equipment (knives, sharp forks, sharp cans and the lids), camp supplies (fuels, repellents, lotions, gas lanterns, matches, hatchet, saw), medicines, and fishing gear (rods, reels, hooks, knives, and bait) out of small children's reach. Always be careful to keep these children away from the campfire. Remember that the coals stay hot long after you are aware that the area is dangerous.

Another important consideration for this age group is making certain they get enough sleep so that they do not get tired and cranky. Naps will have to be worked out as you see best. Besides keeping the child confined at the campsite, a portable crib/playpen is the trick for naps at most recreation spots such as a lake. Put the crib where someone can stay nearby and where it is quiet and shaded. If your child does not settle down easily in such places, you may need to make time in your day to be back at the campsite during his usual naptime. Allow your child to catch needed sleep whenever it fits into the schedule. Try to keep track of just how much sleep your child got in a day, and gear the evening to an appropriate bedtime. The portable crib/playpen is useful for night sleeping too, unless you prefer to have the child sleep with you.

Other equipment needs for toddlers on a camping trip include a stroller suitable for taking on hikes and/or a backpack carrier. The stroller can double as a high chair and as a chair around the campfire. Keep in mind that table meals are a bit awkward for these young children at a campsite picnic table because of the space between the bench and the table. Besides a stroller, a special seat that clamps on the tables, a collapsible high chair, or a walker without wheels are possible solutions. A child age 3 or 4 could make do with either a booster seat or a stack of pillows.

This age group gets dirty quickly by playing on the ground at the campsite. That's not a problem until you decide to go on an outing. You will need to not only change clothes for the outing but also take along an extra set in case the child gets wet. If you want to dress the child for bed early in the evening, you will need to be prepared for that set of clothes to get dirty before he is tucked in. This amounts to two or three daytime outfits and one or two nighttime sets per day. Some of these changes include a bathing suit, shorts, and long pants. So, for five days you might plan on taking two or three bathing suits, five or more overalls, five shorts, and ten or more various types of tops. Include clothes for cold mornings and evenings, such as several sweaters, a jacket, a hat, and even mittens. If you like your child to wear a bib for meals, you might find he is self-conscious about wearing it while camping. A colorful bandanna works wonders here! Fold it in a triangle and tie it at the back of the neck.

Encourage your child's interest in collecting the leaves and rocks around the campsite by providing a container for him—a sandpail is perfect. He can make crayon rubbings with his leaves if you remember to bring along paper (construction paper is nice) and thick crayons. Other good picnic table activities to keep this age group entertained on a rainy day or during a quiet time are coloring books and crayons, scissors, paste, plain paper, and even a few simple puzzles. For more active play, a soft foam ball that does not travel far is ideal.

Since children in this age group can be a handful, your vacation will be more fun when you consider them at every phase. Your recreation will be just as much fun, probably more, with them along; you just need to make sensible choices about the activities they will enjoy.

GRADE-SCHOOL CHILDREN (five to eleven)

Children from age five to eleven make excellent campers. They are eager learners because they like new experiences; they ask questions; they learn through play and like simple tasks that they learn from; they are enthusiastic; they are energetic; and they are good helpers because they like to please. This sounds like a setup for camping, because it is here that the situation is just perfect for all of these attributes. Use the campsite routine for the pragmatic instruction that is unique to camping.

This age group will be willing to treat camping chores as part of the fun. Seize this trait; it is the true camper spirit. Let them participate as much as they can in pitching the tent, building the campfire, fetching water, washing dishes, and learning about the stove and lantern. Even everyday routine chores can be a delight to them when camping. Help them to regard meal preparation, garbage disposal, cleanup, and caring for siblings as recreation. The more they help, the more they develop good camping manners: everyone pitches in. They can participate in doing chores at camp more than at home, because the outdoor vacation standard is the easy way, or any way that gets the job done. Avoid remarks about their methods. If they are functional or thorough enough, just thank the children for the help.

Children at this age level may demonstrate their independence when they show an interest in doing their own packing for a camping trip. Teach them to make a list. Go over the list to be assured that the right things are taken. They will probably think of taking their stuffed animal and toys. Limit the quantity and assure them that you are taking along some activities, too. For a stay of five days, they can get by on one or two sets of pajamas and two outfits a day—one of shorts and one of long pants. Remember, though, that if your child likes to explore and be active, he will need a few extra sets of clothing. Two bathing suits are perfect for any length of stay. Take slip-on shoes for getting up in the night; sandals are nice for some excursions; and two pairs of tennis shoes are standard for any length of stay. Take a warm jacket, sweater, gloves, neck scarf, hat, and long underwear (or substitute tight-fitting pajamas or sweatpants). Plan ahead for hot days and cold nights in many areas.

Be prepared to include this age group at their level in every form of recreation that you enjoy. Ages five to eleven can swim, hike, identify animals, sketch, ride a bicycle, fish, appreciate an ice cream cone, sing, and do almost anything else—except relax! They will love it when you play ball with them on the campground road. (When using the campground road for play, make certain your vision is not blocked by a curve or a hill.) They will also love board and card games in the evening at the table under the light of the lantern. Even simple puzzles are fun, as long as you do not mind losing their pieces, and magazines and books provide an additional quiet-time or rainy day occupation.

Campfires will captivate these children for the fellowship it provides. Cuddle with them, read or tell stories, and sing with them.

Because this age group likes to be active and independent, they will leave the campsite on their own fairly frequently. Be safe, and take precaution against your child getting lost. Give each child a simple whistle to wear around the neck. Explain carefully to the child that the whistles are for emergencies only and that playing with them disturbs other campers. Blows in series of three are an emergency signal.

OLDER CHILDREN AND TEENAGERS

Teenagers and twelve-year-olds may not be as enthusiastic about camping as their younger siblings, or they may think they have outgrown it. They often have definite opinions about what is fun and have individual and high-interest priorities about how to spend their time. There will have to be something in the vacation that they look forward to. Make certain there are activities of particular interest to them near the campground. This may mean that you have to give up your first-choice destination. Or it might be that taking along a friend is more enjoyable than a particular activity, and it would be wise for you to accommodate this wish if possible. Try to include their preferences in the trip in such a way that everyone stays together as much as possible, or, in the case of bigger families, stays together in split groups. For example, everyone can go to the lake while some swim, some water ski, and some play at the shore. Everyone can eat lunch together.

When teenagers do a little something alone—bike ride, go fishing, hike—it is not the time to worry about supervision. Your customary family policy on this subject will not change much for the vacation. Rather than concentrating on supervision, be grateful that you are all together.

Enjoy the young-adult aspect of older children by including them in the planning process. This age group may find that researching areas is exciting especially because it gives them a role in the decision-making process and a tangible sense of contribution. During this planning time you can get the vacation off to a good start by applying adult wisdom to topics with conflicting views. Keep in mind good listening skills and be upbeat, relaxed, cooperative, and understanding.

Twelve-year-olds and teenagers are likely to take care of their own packing. Give them an idea of the weather to expect and the activities on the itinerary. They probably will be interested in taking something special along for recreational pursuits: a bicycle; a good-looking swim suit; swim apparatus such as goggles and fins; water skis; a camera; a fishing pole; an air mattress for the water; magazines for the hammock; their own tent; and spending money! They do not need any of these, but they will appreciate the special treatment. What you can do and what is prudent to do will be the guide.

Teenagers also can be involved in meal planning. By this age, many of them have developed some individual preferences about their eating habits. While some want bulk, others want low-calorie food. This may mean you will have to take special foods along for them. Involve them in the food planning. You also might give them responsibility for planning and cooking a few of the family's meals. You might even let them be in charge of some creative cooking, such as of a stew cooked all day in a fire pit, if that enthuses them.

The more your teenagers and preteens feel involved in the camping trip by helping with the planning, the cooking, and even in keeping a travel log of the trip, the more they are likely to enjoy it.

A final word of caution: Beware of the hype in vacation planning that infers that all troubles will go away when the family drives off into the woods. It is wise to make a point of instilling reality into your vacation talk so that your children are not susceptible to an anticlimax at some point during the camping trip. There may be some disappointments in the weather; someone might not feel well one day; and someone may be unhappy to learn that certain nagging responsibilities like keeping one's belongings together are just as important on a camping trip as at home.

If everyone knows what to expect on the trip and has participated in its planning, it is likely that they will find it a memorable experience.

3

Equipment

Camping equipment has only one real purpose—to make the trip as enjoyable as possible. Lack of equipment and information about it can cause undue strain. Make your vacation pleasant by taking the necessary equipment and by knowing how to use it.

You may always prefer to stay at an organized, established campground that provides all possible amenities. But some people like to master their camping skills and then go to a campground without amenities such as plumbing and nearby stores or go back-packing into wilderness areas where camping is permitted (but nothing is provided for campers).

Whichever way you prefer to camp, in the long run, equipment is the key. But you do not need to be burdened with a lot of flashy or complicated equipment. This chapter covers basic, practical information for the average beginning camper and provides just enough background for your shopping trips. You can also broaden your knowledge about marketing trends by talking to clerks at several sporting goods stores. Retailers' catalogs are another good source of basic information. Check the appendix for names and addresses of suppliers of camping equipment.

Renting or borrowing equipment is another option for your first few trips. This will give you a chance to test both the equipment and the sport. Many camping and recreational stores have rental services where you can get some of the basics.

COST OF EQUIPMENT

To measure the true cost of camping equipment, you have to spread

15

your investment over many years, taking into consideration the number of camping trips you have been able to take instead of staying in a motel or hotel.

Estimated Costs of Essential Equipment

EQUIPMENT	ESTIMATED COST
Sleeping bag	$75–175
Foam pad or air mattress	10–50
Tent	70–350
Camp stove	40–60
Ice chest	40
Propane lantern	20–30
Folding water container	5
Flashlight	10
First-aid kit	10–50
Ground cover	10–50

Estimated Costs of Helpful Equipment

EQUIPMENT	COST
Cooking and eating utensils (bring from home)	$25
Dining fly	25–100
Catalytic heater	40
Portable toilet	10–60
T.V. table(s)	8–20
Folding table	20–50
Saw	15
Shovel	7
Hatchet	10–30
Pocket knife	15–55
Recreational gear	(prices vary depending on recreational preference)
Picnic tote	15
Hammock	10–25

GROUP EQUIPMENT

Shopping should be fun because it stirs up enthusiasm for the trip. Children enjoy this phase, too.

Read the instructions for every item purchased. Keep these manuals and any other information for each product in your camp file.

Keep the gear in the original boxes. If the box is not covered with a glossy paper or is not extra thick, varnish it with shellac. If needed, glue or tape together the flaps that make the bottom and reinforce the corners with tape. Keeping everything secure and protected in the original box, which is usually a good fit, keeps gear in good shape for years and years of storage and traveling to and from the campground.

The following is basic information for the essential items needed on your first trip as well as priority luxury items that can wait for subsequent trips.

Roof Rack or Top Carrier

A roof rack or top carrier for your car is a good place for the tent, the stove, sleeping bags, camp chairs, and foam pads. It keeps baggage from clogging up the passenger space. Top carriers come in numerous styles. Find the one that suits your car and your packing needs.

Use it wisely. Keep the weight from 100 to 200 pounds. When you turn a sharp corner, all the weight up top exerts a sizable amount of tug, making it a little tougher to drive. Place the top carrier well forward to help achieve balance because much of your weight is already toward the rear of the car. If your car sags from overload, try putting on air shocks at the rear of the car.

Utility Trailer

The utility trailer makes packing easy and driving comfortable while allowing for more passenger space in the car. (It can be used for hauling jobs at home, too.) Buy or rent one.

When towing a utility trailer be sure to: balance the weight evenly from front to back; hitch it properly; make sure the lights function properly; properly secure the load with a tarp (for a utility trailer); and make sure the tires are in good condition.

The utility trailer

You will need a permanent trailer hitch installed on your car, and the following connections between the car and the trailer: brake lights, turn signal lights, backup lights, safety chain connection between the car and the trailer, and special rearview mirrors.

Tent

A tent is an essential piece of equipment for camping in a campground, unless you are going to use a recreational vehicle.

Choose a tent carefully. It will be your home for years and years. When thinking about a size to choose, decide if the entire family will sleep in it or if the older children will have an auxiliary tent. Consider the square footage along with the manufacturer's recommendations on sleeping capacity. There is an advantage to getting a tent a little larger than you think you need. It is easier to use up space than to create it, and it is nice to have your clothes kept handy in the tent. It hardly requires more time to set up a larger tent, and it takes very little added space in the car when collapsed.

The breathability and waterproofing of a tent are important factors. When a tent fabric is breathable, moisture cannot build within the tent. However, a breathable fabric is not waterproof, it alone does not keep out the rain. Moreover, a waterproof fabric does not breathe, so the tent then needs another means of ventilation. You want to find a tent that provides for both breathability and waterproofing.

Select either a dome tent, cabin tent, or an A-frame tent. The dome tent is rounded, just as its name implies. Its poles are pushed through sleeves on the outside of the tent, going from one side of the tent, over the top, and down the other. This pole structure makes the tent keep its shape. The top-of-the-line models usually have guy lines and stakes, which provide stability in windy weather. Another top-of-the-line tent is the geodesic dome tent in which the poles criss-cross at midway points as well as at the top. Because the poles intersect each other, they help give the structure greater strength. The fabric for dome tents is usually not waterproof, so waterproofing is accomplished by a fitted waterproof covering referred to as a rainfly. It goes over the tent and is anchored down. Look for a design where the rainfly does not touch the tent fabric; this space is necessary to allow the tent to breathe.

The cabin tent is considered a family tent because it has more space for the money. It is rectangular in shape. Look for a design where you set up the pole frame, which can stand alone while you snap, clasp, or hook on the tent. It is a little more difficult to put the poles through sleeves and then connect the pole segments. Usually the cabin tent is waterproofed in one of two ways. The actual tent fabric can be waterproof; in that case, ventilation is provided by windows. In other tents, the tent ceiling can be a thin (gossamer) fabric that breathes, and the sides can be waterproof. In this case, the tent comes with a rainfly that covers the top.

The A-frame tent is the oldest tent shape. It has been called the pup tent and the army tent. Over the years its basic design has been updated, making it an option for a smaller family tent (up to a roomy four-man size). Today, sturdy aluminum poles with shock cord, a tight rounded fit at the top, and sleeves at the seams for the pole to run through have changed the old appearance so it no longer looks

The pop-up tent (with rainfly)

like the traditional army tent. This design comes in a breathable fabric with a rainfly.

All styles come with either aluminum or fiberglass poles. Shock cording keeps the pole sections together and adds some extra strength. All the best poles are shock-corded. When fiberglass poles break, they tend to shatter. Although aluminum poles can bend, they are less likely to break. Check for the quality of aluminum; or, in the case of the cabin tent, a heavier, bigger pole might be used.

Always look for quality construction. Look for double-stitched seams and reinforcement at the stress points. This could be an extra thickness sewn to the points where the tent and the pole connect.

When shopping for a tent, you want reliable information, an opportunity to see tents made by quality manufacturers, and a chance to see the tent standing. Usually this is all accomplished at a better sporting goods store.

Before taking your tent on a camping trip, set it up in your back yard. While one person sprays it all over with a hose, another person should stand inside the tent to check for leaks at the seams. Mark the leaks with a felt-tip pen. Let the tent dry out and then use a seam sealer, which is available at camping supply stores. Do this checking and repairing about every two years.

TENT CARE - At the campsite open the windows of the tent daily so that air can circulate through it. The inside of a tent can get damp from the condensation of moisture, even in dry weather. Airing the tent gives this moisture a chance to dry out.

Sweep the tent interior daily with a whisk broom to protect it from punctures caused by the dirt and twig particles that are tracked in (even with a small rug at the entrance).

If you have to pack the tent in the rain or while it is wet or damp, set it up and dry it out when the weather clears up. This will save the fabric from mildew. You should never pack away for storage a tent that is the least bit damp.

After every camping trip, turn the tent inside out and shake it. Turn it back to fold it and pack it away. The outside of the tent usually does not need to be washed, but do wash it when you see leaf sap, bird droppings, and food spillage. Simply sponge it with a mild soap, rinse thoroughly, and dry.

If you get a puncture or tear in the tent fabric, use a patch kit or a piece of ripstop nylon with adhesive backing that is sold for this purpose at camping supply stores.

Auxiliary Tent(s)

Older children like to have their own shelter. They will enjoy pitching and breaking their own camp. It puts a new and exciting slant on camping for them. Also, the auxiliary tent solves the problem of an overcrowded family tent. It is not an essential piece of equipment for all families, however. If you do decide to buy one, choose an inexpensive A-frame tent.

Ground Cover (tarp)

Put a lightweight ground cover (tarp or plastic) under your tent. This will preserve the tent floor, which is often too thin to prevent twigs and little rocks from piercing through it when you move around. Also, it is easier to clean the tarp than the tent.

A piece of polyethylene that is six mils thick (thousandths of an inch, some use three mils) works fine and is about a fourth of the cost of a tarp. This sheet of plastic comes in rolls at hardware stores. You can get a ten-foot width cut to the length you want. Get two if your tent is wider than ten feet. Or, you can get a tougher tarp at a camping store or department store.

Camp Stove

A camp stove is standard camping equipment because it gives instant, steady heat, similar to your range at home. Although it is part of the fun to cook over a campfire, a camp stove is more convenient.

Tent camping and backpacking require different stoves and fuels. For backpacking you need something light for both the stove and the fuel. A propane canister of fuel is too heavy and bulky. Instead, use white gas, kerosene, or alcohol. There are stoves that will take all three fuels. Check at a camping store for the stove that fits your needs.

Tent camping calls for propane or white gas. Propane comes in

A propane campstove

convenient and easy-to-use cylinders (canisters). One cylinder burns for about six hours. Some people think that canisters are too expensive. You can go with a refillable bulk tank, which can be refilled at most RV campgrounds and at RV supply stores. They are an economical source of propane fuel.

Although white gas is the most economical source of fuel, it is not as easy to use. It does not come in a pressurized can. You fill the gas tank by pouring in the liquid, and then pumping air pressure into the tank.

For simple, relaxed, beginning camping, go with propane fuel in the high-pressure cylinders. To operate them, you just turn the valve and touch a match to the burner plate. Read the instructions for your make and model.

You should know the basic safety precautions about your propane gas stove.

• When there is a leak, there will be an "off-smelling" odor, a little like garlic. In the case of a leak, check all joints (couplings). Do this by feeling around the joints for coldness. Look for frost. When you tighten the connection, wear gloves because the chill is so intense it can cause frostbite to your fingers. Liquid propane gives off so much thermal energy on contact with the atmosphere that any material it touches almost immediately goes to forty degrees below zero.

A less hazardous way of checking the joints is by pouring a liquid soap (detergent) solution of about four parts water to one part soap on all joints. Bubbles will form where there is a leak.

• Never throw empty propane cylinders into a fire or fire pit. THEY EXPLODE.

• Never operate the stove in an enclosed area, such as the tent, where there is insufficient ventilation. It will create poisonous gases.

• Never refuel a hot stove.

• Never set oversized pots on the stove.

• Never enclose a stove with aluminum foil.

Lantern

A two-mantle propane lantern is essential for camping. It will provide light in the evening while you are washing dinner dishes, playing games at the table, and getting ready for bed. One lantern is fine for the first trip, but you may want to bring more later.

Have an extra supply of mantles because they are fragile and break easily. When you tie on a new mantle, leave the fuel off, and burn the mantle until only ash remains. Carefully replace the glass. Light it with wooden matches. Follow the manufacturer's instructions.

A propane lantern

Your light should not intrude into neighboring areas. Use discretion when setting the brightness of your lantern. Other campers may get some of the glow. When in doubt be moderate with the light.

Catalytic Heater

During the summer in the mountains, it gets cold at night and in the morning. You will love the luxury of a heater for dressing and undressing. But you are not likely to need it on a summertime trip to a lake or ocean.

There is no open flame with a catalytic heater, and if it gets knocked over, fuel does not spill. However, observe the following precautions: Keep everything off the heater while it is glowing; do not allow clothing or bedding near it; keep items two feet away from the front and the sides; ventilate the tent (the heater consumes oxygen); light the heater outside; and follow the manufacturer's instructions.

Ice Chest

An insulated ice chest can store food almost as efficiently as your refrigerator. Look for one with sturdy handles, hinges, and latch. The handles should be easy to grasp. There should be an end drain with a screw cap and a chain to keep it from getting lost. Some chests have removeable water jugs to freeze ahead of time and screw into the lid.

Two small chests rather than one large one give you several advantages: They are lighter and easier to pack into the car or trailer. A small one is convenient for side trips. Food can be divided between them according to temperature needs and access needs.

Dining Canopy

Campers like having a dining canopy or fly over the picnic table to keep it shaded from the sun, clean from droppings, and protected from rain. The average size is twelve feet square. It comes with five poles; the center pole, which is propped in the middle of the picnic

The dining canopy (fly)

table, keeps the canopy about two feet higher than the corners. The four corner poles are about six feet high and are anchored with poles and ropes that you have to either fasten to the ground with a stake or tie to a nearby tree. The dining canopy comes in a variety of prices and materials; the quality at the lower price is adequate, but you can get a better composition tarp, better grommet construction, and sturdier poles if you pay more.

It is best to have about three people to set up the canopy. The center pole goes through a grommet in the center of the canopy, then it is propped in the middle of the table. Have one person hold onto it. The second person should set up a corner pole, then the third person should hold onto the diagonally opposite corner to pull it taut. Now set up the pole in that corner. Set up the other two corner poles in the same way. With one or two people available to work, you will have to improvise a system that works for you. The canopy also can be tied with ropes through its corner grommets to nearby trees.

Before you put away the dining canopy, be certain it is dry and clean.

Folding Table

A folding table is not an essential piece of camping equipment, but it is very helpful. The sturdy picnic tables at public campsites seat six to eight, but dining will be cramped if part of the table must be used to prepare the meal. Bring a folding table to hold the stove and supplies and to provide working space. Be sure the table is sturdy so that there is no danger of collapsing or tipping. A second folding table can be used for dishwashing, if you wish.

Camp Chairs

Take a folding chair for each family member. You will use them for the evening campfires, relaxing around the campsite, eating meals around the fire and much more. Get whatever folding chair suits you. Some sit lower, like a beach chair, which are more comfortable in the sun and fine for the campsite. The small chairs are a good choice for children up to about eight years old.

Bring plenty of camp chairs. Everyone needs a comfortable place to sit.

Portable Toilet

For small children and those who have to get up in the middle of the night, the portable toilet is a wonderful luxury to keep in the main tent.

If you have traveling space for a self-contained chemical toilet, they are the answer. Follow the manufacturer's instructions for filling it with a disinfectant solution and for emptying. If you are short on space, consider a simple portable commode. Keep a disinfectant in it.

Pocketknife

Some campers like a pocketknife. You can get the single-blade kind or the Swiss army knife—a term for any multitool pocketknife. These feature handy accessories such as a screwdriver, scissors, tweezers, and a magnifying glass, depending on the brand and model.

Keep your knife sharp. You will see a variety of sharpening options at the stores and in the catalogs. If you sharpen with a diamond stone, use water on the stone to float away the steel particles, which clog the pores of the stone and reduce its cutting efficiency. The stone comes in coarse for the initial work and fine for the final smoothing work. If you use a sharpening stone kit, it will have a hard stone for initial work, a soft stone for the final cutting edge, lubricating oil, and instructions.

If you buy a stone without instructions, follow this procedure. Apply two or three drops of oil (water for the diamond) to the stone. Lift the back of the blade so that the blade is at a twenty-degree angle. Stroke the blade across the stone from the back to the point, first on one side and then on the other, flipping the blade with each stroke. Bear down slightly. Make sure that you maintain a twenty-degree angle. Clean the stone and the blade frequently, applying more lubricant during the sharpening process.

Hatchet

A hatchet is a small, short-handled ax, which is used with one hand. It is fine for splitting kindling—your main camping use. For producing campfire wood, use the hatchet in conjunction with a saw. Use the hatchet as a splitting wedge. Split wood burns faster than whole logs. Just keep splitting, and you have kindling. Never anchor the wood that you are splitting with your foot or your hand. Prop the log on its end and against another log or a rock.

With a one-piece hatchet, you will not have to worry about the head flying off the handle, but they have a tendency to vibrate. Shop around to see if you can meet the quality of a wooden-handled hatchet in a one-piece style. Look for: a heavy head; a quality-steel head (not cast iron); and good balance. Most hardware stores and nice department stores carry high-quality tools. Camping tools can also be purchased through mail-order camping supply companies.

If you do get a two-piece hatchet with a wooden handle, test the tightness of the handle by holding the tool with the head hanging down and by pounding on the end of the handle. Mark where the head is on the handle. Now, turn the hatchet in the other direction with the head on top. Being careful not to pound on the tool's head, pound on the handle coming out of the head. Mark where the head is on the handle. If the head moves on the handle, it is too loose for safety. To tighten the head, insert a shim into the gap. With the head up, drive a wedge or metal shim into the gap. If some of the wooden wedge protrudes from the eye of the head, cut it off with a saw.

Keep your hatchet sharp. A dull hatchet is dangerous because it can bounce off wood and hit you—a sharp hatchet digs into the wood. To sharpen the hatchet, use a file and a whetstone (sharpening stone) and wear gloves. Wedging the head (cutting edge up) is not safe because you file into the edge of the hatchet. Instead, lay the hatchet flat on a stump or table with just a quarter inch of edge showing over the side. Now when you file into the blade, your fingers will hit the side of the stump or table before the steel. File downward, first on one side of the head and then on the other. Go about one inch from the edge, and get a uniform taper. Finish off with the coarse side of the whetstone, using straight strokes as you did with the file. Now use the fine side of the stone with rotary strokes.

Always keep your hatchet sheathed when not in use. A small pocket on the sheath makes a good storage place for the whetstone. While in use at a campsite, you can drive the hatchet into a log or stump. Position the handle high so that no one will trip over it.

Saw

In many state and national campgrounds, you are not allowed to gather firewood, so no doubt you will buy some precut pieces from the ranger station or a local store. However, when you can gather wood, or when you bring logs from home, you will want to cut it. A saw will cut two to three times more wood in a given period of time and with less effort than a hatchet.

A good camper's saw is either the bow saw or the folding saw. The bow saw resembles the buck saw, which is a larger, lumberman's saw. The folding saw is handy for campers. If you do not have a folding model, keep the blade masked (covered). You can rig up a cover with a piece of cardboard folded over the length of the teeth and fastened with several strong clips.

Use your saw to cut logs into short lengths, and use your hatchet to split these. Use easy, smooth strokes, pulling the saw back and forth the entire length of the blade without downward pressure. The weight of the saw is the pressure you want.

When the blade gets dull, either put on a new one or sharpen it at home. Keep spare blades to replace dull, bent, or broken ones.

Improve the cutting performance and prevent the blade from rusting by wiping it with gasoline or alcohol.

Shovel

A shovel is used for cleaning out the campfire area and the outdoor grill. And, if you do hot-ash and/or pit cooking, you will need a shovel to move the coals. Get a short-handled or folding style. The folding shovel has a pointed blade. Some short-handled shovels have a flat blade.

Travel File

Use a small letter-size file with a handle, a latch, and some folders. Get off to a good start and keep all camping information here—road maps, campground reservations, brochures, travel folders, campground directories, trip budget book, and the instructions and parts lists for your equipment.

First-Aid Kit

To make your own first-aid kit, see the chapter on first aid. Ready-made kits come in various styles and price ranges. Shop around. This is an easy item to find. You might want to consider the unique design put out by the American Red Cross. It includes individual foil packets for special treatments as well as various important accessories in a 10-by-12-inch pillow. The instructions are printed right on the kit and repeated on the packets.

Kitchen Gear Checklist

Pack your kitchen gear after referring to the chapter on food and your own menu lists. You will find that you do not need every one of these items on every trip; for instance, if you do not choose to do any pit cooking, you will not need a bean pot.

- Individual plate, cup, knife, fork, spoon, and bowl (nested camp sets available)
- Assortment of pans, kettles, and lids (nested camp sets available)
- Griddle or frying pan
- Large or deep kettle for boiling water on campfire
- Stirring and serving spoons and forks
- Pancake turner
- Rubber bowl scraper
- Sharp knife
- Grater
- Potato peeler
- Long-handled tongs for foil cooking in campfire
- Kitchen tongs
- Steak knives
- Strainer
- Cutting board
- Hot pads
- Pot holders or oven mitts
- Plastic tablecloth
- Plastic containers with secure lids
- Mixing bowl(s)
- Coffee pot
- Cast-iron bean pot (Dutch oven); season with oil at home before packing
- Cooking forks for campfire (or wire coat hangers or green sticks—as big around as your thumb)

- Charcoal and starter fluid
- Portable barbecue (table top), if one is not provided at your camp-site, or grill
- Fuel for camp stove, lantern, and heater
- Matches in a waterproof container
- Heavy-duty foil for hot-ash cooking
- Paper or plastic garbage bags
- Foil, plastic bags, wax paper, paper towels
- Dish detergent, bar soap, pot scouring pads, sponge, towels
- Chlorine bleach for dishwashing
- Dishpans
- Roll of masking tape to reseal boxes and packages
- Sturdy rubber bands to secure wrapped food
- Food

Smaller Group Items

This list finishes off the basic equipment for the group. These things are not as expensive as the previous listings, but all of the items are important.

- Flashlight(s)
- Folding water carrier
- Hammock (high-priority luxury)
- Recreation items
- Picnic tote
- T.V. tables for eating around the campfire (Individual-size folding tables are available from an RV accessory supplier, and discount stores have good buys in wood sets.)
- Wood (if not available at the ranger station and if you have space and weight capacity)

- Small, lightweight, machine-washable or grass mat entrance rug(s)
- Rope for clothesline
- Clothespins
- Toilet paper for portable toilet
- Small broom, dust broom, or whisk broom
- Work gloves for campsite chores
- Shock (stretch) cords (good in a variety of lengths for such purposes as holding items on the roof rack and for tying around a tree branch for a hook)
- Outdoor thermometer
- Inflator/deflator (plugs into car cigarette lighter for plastic water loungers, toys, and/or air mattresses)
- Water purification tablets (for backpacking and/or nonestablished campsites)
- Battery-operated radio

INDIVIDUAL EQUIPMENT

There are a few things that each individual must have for comfort and fun. Remember that these personal items make wonderful birthday, Christmas, and graduation presents. Plan ahead, and your family can gear up for camping.

Sleeping bag

Each individual must have a sleeping bag that is warm and dry. Choose your sleeping bag carefully, and get the best you can afford.

Basically, there are two initial choices—a down or a synthetic-filled bag. A down bag is superior in every category except retention of wetness and price.

When choosing a fill, keep in mind how the bag works: Its purpose is to insulate, to keep in your body heat, and not to give heat. Loft (any porous material, such as down or polyester fiberfill, with high resilience and compressibility) gives the bag insulation. Its effectiveness is measured by thickness, so the more loft in a bag, the warmer the bag.

Traditionally, loft is measured by thoroughly shaking out the zipped-up bag, laying it on the floor, letting it settle for several minutes, then measuring the distance from the floor to the top of the bag. The measurement should be taken at the midsection of the bag where your lower chest would be. Loft range is from one and one-half inches (lightweight, summer) to eight inches (expedition).

How much loft do you need? A few suppliers use laboratory tests to scientifically determine the comfort ratings of their bags—the outdoor temperature at which the bag will be comfortable—and these ratings have proven highly accurate. You may already know if you are a cold person or a warm person and can make reasonable adjustments to the standardized ratings, if you wish. If you sleep cold, add five to ten degrees to the rating. If you sleep warm, subtract five to ten degrees.

Understanding this, you will realize the importance of checking the construction of the bag—a well-constructed bag keeps heat from escaping. A good down bag has baffles (compartments that hold the insulation in place) inside an inner and outer shell to prevent the down from shifting. If the bag were simply stitched through, it would be only as effective as the thickness at the sewn-through stitching. That would not be very warm because all of the heat would leave through the stitching holes. Look for good baffle construction.

If you choose a synthetic bag, make sure the polyester fiberfill batting goes to the edges and is quilted in small sections to prevent shifting. Advancements and changes occur all the time, so research the market.

If you need to use extra bedding, use wool blankets. Wool retains heat and allows the body's moisture to escape so that the bedding is not dampened. Do not cover the outside of the bag with rubber, plastic, or any other material that is completely waterproof. Waterproof covers are nearly airtight and would trap body moisture.

The top cover of a sleeping bag must be porous enough for the moisture-laden air to escape.

You may want to insert a liner into your bag to keep it clean and (with some polyester blend fabrics) add some warmth. It is also helpful to have a liner fabric that is slick or smooth to prevent tangling when you wear long underwear or flannel sleepwear.

Sleeping bags come with a stuff sack for travel. Take the bag out of the sack when you arrive at camp and also between uses to allow the filler to attain a full loft. At home, store your sleeping bag draped over a clothes hanger in a closet. When you stuff your bag for travel, do not try to roll or fold it; just stuff it into the sack. Unstuff a bag gently so as not to tear out the baffles. Do not sit on a stuff sack with the sleeping bag inside.

To prevent the zipper of the sleeping bag from catching on the edge of the bag's fabric, zip slowly and carefully. When it does catch, place your thumbs on the cloth on each side of the snag and pry (pull) apart gently to release the snag. If you move the zipper itself, you will only make it worse.

A sleeping bag does not need to be washed after every trip, but it should be aired out before storage. If outdoor airing is not possible, run it through a dryer on an air setting or very low heat. Keep the bag away from direct sunlight or extreme heat. Both will dry out the natural oils in down and destroy the crimp and bonding agents in synthetic fills. While you are camping, remember to air your sleeping bag every day. It may not feel damp, but body moisture is there.

Wash your sleeping bag according to the manufacturer's instructions. The guidelines are a little different for down and synthetic bags.

CLEANING A DOWN BAG - If professionally cleaning it, take your bag to a cleaners that specializes in sleeping bags. They will either dry-clean it with a solvent agreeable to down, or they will wash it.

If you clean the bag yourself, never use a coin-operated machine; the solvents harm the down. The best option is to hand wash your down bag. Use your bathtub and a special soap. Down bag soap is extra mild so it does not take out the natural oils that keep the down fluffed. Find it at a camping supply store. Some people use a very mild soap; never use a detergent.

Prescrub any spots on the outside. Then, because the bag is likely to be dirtiest on the inside, turn it inside out before washing. Use lukewarm water and wash without pulling or lifting on the fabric.

Rinse the bag thoroughly in the bathtub by draining the water repeatedly and by carefully squeezing, pushing, and kneading the soap out of the bag. Never lift the bag up; the weight would damage the fragile baffles. Drain out the water, and press out as much water as you can with the bag remaining flat in the tub. Use a stack of bath towels to blot out water. Then carefully lift the bag out of the tub by cradling it from the underside. Place the bag on a sheet and carry it to a shady spot outside. Make sure the bag is fully supported—flat on the ground—not on a clothesline and turn the bag every so often. It will take from one to four days to get it almost dry. Then complete the drying and fluff it in the dryer on the "no heat" setting, and toss in a couple of tennis balls or a clean sneaker to help break up clumps of down.

CLEANING A SYNTHETIC BAG - Do not dry-clean a synthetic bag. It can either be hand washed or machine washed in a front-loading commercial machine. Use warm or cold water and a very mild soap. Air dry the bag.

Foam Pad, Air Mattress, and/or Cot

Whenever down or synthetic insulation is pressed flat against the ground, it loses nearly all its insulation value because all there is between you and the ground is some crushed feathers or synthetic filling plus very thin nylon. Because of this, most sleeping bags have sixty percent of the insulation on the top half. You need something more underneath.

FOAM PADS - Manufacturers work with two basic types of foam (open cell and closed cell) in making foam pads. There are different types and brands of these two types, and the market is always changing, so talk to store clerks or read labels and catalogs carefully.

The open-cell foam pad has air spaces that make the material cushiony, which is good for a mattress. However, what is not so good is that it is bulky (usually one-and-a-half inches thick) and absorbent, allowing ground dampness in. The absorbency can be taken care of with a cover with a waterproofed nylon bottom and a breathable cotton-polyester top.

The closed-cell pad is compressed so there are no air spaces for ground dampness to seep through. The tiny cells trap a layer of dead air, which acts as an effective insulation. The insulation and the comfort are in proportion to the thickness. A quarter-inch provides enough warmth for the summer, but not much softness. The closed-cell pad is stiff and has to be tied when it is rolled.

SELF-INFLATING MATTRESS - This is an open-cell pad within an air mattress. The foam insulates while the air mattress provides comfort. To inflate it you simply open the valve and unroll the bag; it inflates automatically. (You can blow in more air if desired.) Then close the valve, which traps the air in the foam. It deflates when you open the valve and roll up the pad, forcing out the air.

It is a good idea to make a cotton (any breathable fabric that is not slippery) cover for a self-inflating mattress to protect it from punctures and to prevent it from slipping out from under you. Punctures are pinpoint holes that may deflate the mattress over a period of half a night.

These mattresses require a little extra care. Keep the valve clean and remove any bits of sand or dirt that creep in; most deflations result from a dirty valve that cannot quite close. Be careful to prevent punctures, and take along a patch kit in case you get one.

AIR MATTRESS - This alternative is for comfort, not warmth. An air mattress circulates cold air. When the air moves, the warm body air cools off as it comes into contact with the cold ground. You can use an air mattress in tandem with an insulating pad—a closed-cell foam pad. To prevent slippage of this stack, try anchoring it to your tarp at the corners with carpet tape, which is double sided and very sticky.

You can blow up your air mattress by mouth, with a lightweight foot pump, or a 12-volt inflator/deflator that plugs into your car cigarette lighter. You insert a 12-volt fuse into the electrical system. The valve on the mattress screws in tightly.

The air mattress comes in a vinyl-coated or rubberized fabric. Do not get a plastic mattress. They are made for floating on the water, not outdoor sleeping. Plastic punctures easily and usually has skimpy seams and plastic plugs that pop out.

COT - A cot is not a bad idea for those who want the extra comfort, have a little extra car space, and can spend the extra money. You still need an insulator—closed-cell foam pad. Cots come in compact aluminum models that fold into a small bag not much larger than a sleeping bag.

Clothing and Shoes

You, the consumer, are deluged with viewpoints and varieties to consider when it comes to clothing. Understanding the basic fabrics and the layering system of dressing can help you put it all together to fit your individual needs while camping.

FABRICS - There are too many to list, and new ones continually come onto the market. A rundown on the basics will prevent you from getting confused when you read labels in the stores. Clothing is made of combinations or blends of these basic fabric types.

• Wool traps air, absorbs moisture, and is warm even when it is wet. It can be scratchy. It is resilient and must be washed gently in cold water.

• Cotton absorbs moisture and does not provide insulation when wet. It is soft and easy to wash.

• Silk is warm, even when wet, and light, soft, and elastic. It requires special care.

• Nylon is durable and dries quickly. You will find it used in a blend for thermal underwear, and sometimes it is coated to become waterproof.

•Polypropylene will not absorb water (wicking ability), is lightweight and feels good. It pills, which does not look nice, and it cannot be washed with hot water. Combined with polyester, it is used in outer garments, and it is also used in underwear and socks.

• Acrylic, olefin, and polyester are alike in that they are generic names for a manufactured fiber in which the fiber-forming substance is any long-chain synthetic polymer. They are different in the chemicals used to process them. Acrylic is found in various items, including athletic underwear and sweaters. Olefin is used in blends; one of its uses is in gloves. Polyester is used for water-resistant and breathable outerwear, as well as in thermal underwear, gloves, thin jackets, and more.

LAYERING - The layering principle involves planning the day's ensemble with a number of single-thickness garments (instead of one or two heavy ones) worn over each other so that they can be taken on and off as the temperature varies. You maintain a comfortable body temperature by removing or adding layers. In the heat, shed layers before sweat makes the inner layer damp; in the cold, put on just the right amount *before* you get cold. If you plan the layers right, you can add and subtract clothes anytime during the day and evening for perfect comfort. For example, when camping in the summer in the mountains, it can get cold at night and in the morning, while it is very hot during the afternoon.

In applying layering principles to a summer day in the mountains, you could choose a cotton outfit to wear as the underwear layer. (Shorts could be in a tote if they are not tight fitting.) Then, depending on the weather, put on another underwear layer of traditional long underwear. Put on a clothing layer of shirt and trousers and then an insulating layer of jacket, hat, and gloves. Sometimes there may not be a clear distinction of layers in your outfit, but you should aim to have all the variable temperatures covered. The categories are not spelled out so that you wear all of them; they are for awareness. For example, in the example above, you might not wear an underwear layer, just your usual underwear, and get enough morning and evening warmth out of a jacket and/or sweater. Or, you might use a bathing suit for underwear.

• Underwear layer. This layer must be in a thin, comfortable fabric that can breathe and wick the moisture (in cold weather). This layer can be worn as an outer layer—a long underwear top looks like a tee shirt. Cotton is good during the summer, but not in cold, wet weather. Do not overlook long underwear for cold evenings in the summer. Do not be confused about net undershirts. They are useful because they can be either warm or cool. They are warm with an outer shirt because air traps in the net.

•Clothing layer. For family camping activities, this layer translates into your usual outfits. Sweat pants are convenient because they can be slipped off or on over shoes.

• Insulating layer. This layer provides warmth when basic clothing is insufficient. It includes sweater, jacket, hat, gloves, and neck scarf.

• Protective or shell layer. This layer is important because it protects against wet, wind, and sun. Even an automobile camper, who can take cover in a tent or car, needs rain gear. It may be raining when you are packing up to go home. Take care that everyone in the family stays dry. A combination of wet, cold, and wind can cause hypothermia, and being wet and cold can bring on the common cold. Your rain gear can be something inexpensive; even a heavy-duty plastic lawn and leaf or garbage bag, with a hole cut for the head, works.

There are four categories of fabrics in this protective layer, based on their varying capabilities: (1) Some fabrics are windproof and breathable. This could be a nylon jacket that has not been water-proofed. Good when you foresee no rain. (2) Some fabrics are wind-proof and waterproof but not breathable. This could be a plastic slicker. Good when you foresee more rain than sweat. (3) Some fabrics are water-repellent, windproof, and breathable. This garment might be in Gore-Tex® fabric. Good when you foresee more mist and drip than hard rain and know that you will be sweating. (4) Some fabrics are waterproof, windproof, and breathable. Good when you want, and can afford, all the capabilities of a fabric. This could be Thinsulate® or Gore-Tex® fabric.

Plan ahead what you need from your outer layer so that you will be sure to take what you need for the weather conditions.

Do not forget a hat and gloves with this layer. When you are cold, an uncovered head can lose a third of the body's heat production. Get a stocking hat that can be worn to bed when it is cold. In the sun, a broad-rimmed hat protects your face, neck, and scalp from sunburn and your eyes from glare.

Bring along a couple of pairs of shoes. Regular tennis shoes (sneakers), moccasins, or a comfortable light or even sturdy pair of sandals are perfect for around the camp. You might also want something to wear on your feet in the shower.

Smaller and High-priority Luxury Items

Many of these items contribute to a more enjoyable trip.

- Sunglasses (polarized)
- Insect repellent (products with N.N-diethyl-meta toluamide—deet—are effective)
- Pillow (bedpillow or stuff sack filled with clothes)
- Backpack
- Watch
- Camera
- Towels and washcloth
- Personal toiletries
- Spare shoelaces
- Chapstick
- Sun lotion
- Sunscreen
- Bathing suit, life jacket
- Binoculars

- Compass
- Writing supplies and notebook
- Musical instruments
- Songbooks
- Reading material
- Money
- Ditty bag (cloth sack, with drawstring enclosure for children's treasures, pick-up-games, underwear, toiletries)

4

Recreational Vehicle Camping

There are many people who enjoy the out-of-doors and the family togetherness that a camping trip provides, but they do not want to be in a tent. They like the pleasures of a bed and a private bathroom, the convenience of a refrigerator and electric lights, and the ability to go away without working to pack their supplies in their car. For them, a recreational vehicle (RV) is the way to go camping. Even the advanced camper or the backpacker sometimes chooses to drive up to a trailhead in an RV using it as a point of departure. RVs are here to stay.

ADVANTAGES AND DISADVANTAGES

If you can afford to consider a recreational vehicle, weigh the advantages and disadvantages carefully.

Advantages

In an RV you can enjoy many of the same things that tent camper and a backpacker enjoys, but with more comfort, privacy, and ease.

The comforts vary with the size of the vehicle. They can be elaborate, with air conditioning, a warm shower, a good mattress, television, stereo, complete kitchen conveniences, and heating and lighting—all without setting up! In an RV you are not restricted to camping only in pleasant and warm weather; you can camp practically year-round.

If you do not like others watching you eat, cook, and keep "house," an RV allows you to be social, with the option of being private.

43

With an RV you can choose long destinations without considering motel stops, and you can take a vacation spontaneously.

An RV minimizes the stress and work of packing. Just put your food and clothing into cupboards; fill up the gas tank, and take off. Once the rig is outfitted, it is just about permanently packed and ready to go.

At your destination, setting up camp with a house vehicle is simple. Back into the campsite; unhitch, if it is a trailer; hook up to water, electricity, and sewer sources, if they are available; level your rig, and enjoy the area. It's a cinch.

Disadvantages

An RV is a big investment in money and upkeep. The cost of the campsite gear is a bargain compared to an RV, and the maintenance is much less. For most people, this cost difference is so great that they could not take a vacation at all without the inexpensive option of tent camping.

If you invest in an RV, you will want to keep it nice, and that takes a great deal of care, everything from washing windows, counters, and walls to lining drawers and scrubbing and waxing large exterior surfaces.

Although many people do not mind towing a trailer or driving a motor home, there are disadvantages. It is an extra driving strain, slower, and more expensive in fuel.

RECREATIONAL VEHICLE TYPES

Begin with an open view as to which style of vehicle will best suit your needs. Within that type there are variations in size and luxury. Get practical and current information from brochures, publications, and dealers; apply your needs and budget to those facts. Here is a description of six basic styles.

Folding Camping Trailer or Tent Trailer

The tent trailer is a utility-trailer–type base with a collapsible tent constructed on it. When set up, it can be very basic or be equipped with a variety of amenities. Some tent trailers have a table, seats that turn into beds, and a canopy. Larger, more expensive models may also include a compartment with a tub or shower and potty, an electric range and refrigerator, and wiring for a stereo system. They usually sleep from four to eight people.

The tent trailer

Tent trailers are easy to tow, a snap to set up, and more economical than other RVs because the gas mileage is better. They are easier to set up than a tent, and they offer space to store gear both when traveling and between trips.

Travel Trailer

Usually a travel trailer is a self-contained trailer with full facilities that can be used for days without connection to outside utilities such as water, electricity, or sewage. They cannot be pulled by small cars, but require a larger family car, van, or pickup truck. When figuring the towing ability and the gas mileage, take into account a fully loaded trailer.

The travel trailer is handy because when you arrive at camp and unhitch from the tow vehicle, you can use that vehicle for errands and sightseeing. The trailer itself is easy to maintain because it does not have a motor (which means it depreciates more slowly and is a good investment).

The travel trailer

Fifth-Wheeler

The fifth-wheeler has dual tires at the rear, four in all—the hitch on the bed of the pickup truck is considered the fifth wheel. This fixed pivot point makes it far more maneuverable than other trailers; it handles easily on the road and backs into a campsite easily.

More than half of the states allow passengers to ride inside (with an intercom) because its hitch is not likely to come undone, and it has more safety and stability on the road than the other trailers.

The raised section over the hitch makes space for a bedroom large enough for twin beds or a queen-size bed complete with bed-side tables.

Hooking and unhooking the trailer is easy, because the engaging is visible through the rear window of the truck. The towing vehicle becomes free for errands and excursions.

The fifth-wheeler

Van Conversion

A modified van (van conversion) may have changes in windows, carpeting, paneling, custom seats, and accessories. A van camper can have a sleeping area, kitchen, toilet facilities, 110-volt hookup, freshwater storage, water hookup, a top extension to provide more head room, and a side tent.

Vans can pull a boat or trailer while providing passenger comfort. They seat from seven to twelve people and sleep from two to four people. (See illustration next page)

Truck Camper (Pickup Camper)

A truck camper can range in size from the cargo space of a pickup truck covered with a low shell to a full living unit affixed to the bed or chassis of a truck. It can have an electric or a gas refrigerator, a water tank with sink and pump toilet, and twin beds or a queen-size bed complete with bedside tables.

The van conversion

The truck camper

A truck camper is easy to drive, and it is legal to ride in the back. It is not easy to jack the camper off the pickup. You might want to carry mopeds or bicycles or tow a small car for errands and excursions. Most truck campers have plenty of power for this extra towing.

The Motor Home

Some motor homes are built on a metal bed that extends behind a truck engine and resembles a bus; others are built directly onto a heavy-duty truck chassis with sleeping quarters up over the cab.

They can have dozens of interior options. The passengers can ride in the back with accessibility to and from the cab. They are always self-powered and are sturdy enough to tow a small car for errands and excursions.

Although motor homes unburden the take off and arrival of a camping trip, they are a big investment in the initial purchase, maintenance, and gas mileage.

The motor home

RENTING A RECREATIONAL VEHICLE

If you are considering purchasing a certain type of motor home or trailer, rent one first to see if you really enjoy RV travel and that particular vehicle. Many RV dealers offer rentals with the hope that the rental will lead to a sale. Some will apply the rental fees against the purchase.

RV rentals have turned into big business. Check the Yellow Pages under Camper Rentals, Trailer Rentals, and Motor Home Rentals. Another source of rental information is *Who's Who in RV Rentals*, a directory published by the Recreation Vehicle Rental Association (RVRA). This book includes services, prices, and a description of the available RVs. Write RVRA, 3251 Old Lee Highway, Fairfax, VA 22030.

When renting be sure to allow time for a thorough orientation of the unit. Have the rental agent instruct you carefully and take you out on a test drive before you sign the contract. Learn to manage the waste-disposal system, the generator, the plumbing hookup, and the electrical connections in the campgrounds. Know where to put the gasoline. Learn how to operate the microwave and all the features unique to the unit itself.

The off-season rates are usually from September 15 to May 15. Make your reservations during those months so that you have a good selection and are not rushed to accept any rate from any agency.

Most RV rental dealers expect you to pay for everything in advance, including an estimated mileage fee and a damage deposit. This usually includes the insurance, but check the deductible, which can run as high as five hundred dollars. Find out who pays for the propane and toilet chemicals.

An RV breakdown can spoil your vacation. Rent from an agency that keeps the rigs in good condition. Some national RV rental agencies have twenty-four–hour road service (with a toll-free 800 number). This is one good reason to be careful about or avoid renting an RV from an individual.

GEAR

The RVs' large size should not tempt you to take along all the paraphernalia you use at home. Keep it plain and simple to avoid clutter and maintenance, as well as added weight that increases gasoline consumption.

Add mechanical tools and cleaning supplies to your packing list. Be careful to include the items that your particular model needs; check the owner's manual.

Make up a special tool box starting with this basic list.

• Hammer

• Vice grip

• Assorted screwdrivers

• Crescent and socket wrenches

• Universal joint adapter

• Electrical supplies (circuit tester, crimper, stripper, electrical tape)

• Oil

• Glue, contact cement

• Towline (rope, chain, cable with hooks on both ends)

Keep the towline in a special place for emergencies. If you use a rope, be sure it is strong enough and tie a bowline knot that is easy to undo.

Cleaning tools include:

• Vacuum cleaner and crevice attachment

• Nonabrasive bathroom cleaners

• All-purpose cleaner

• Long-handled brush for the outside

• Broom

You will have to clean:

• Screens

• Furnace compartment and duct vents

• Air-conditioner grill

• Window coverings and windows

• Upholstery

• Walls and ceiling

• Exterior

• Drawers, cupboards, and closets

• Door mats

Check the following items (you may want to make a checklist, which includes other things) for proper working order and adjustment: fire extinguisher and smoke alarm; side mirrors; trailer's rear lights; tire air and tread; inside items and secured drawers and cupboards.

RV gear sometimes requires special handling. For example, keep the refrigerator door open between trips or at storage time. Do not transport a propane cylinder in a position other than the one in which it is used. Upright cylinders, which are found on most trailers, should be carried upright; horizontal cylinders, common on motor homes, should be transported in a horizontal position. Cylinders either empty or full should never be allowed to roll around or to be tipped over.

PACKING

Keep the weight down. Water is very heavy, so keep it to a minimum. Load the rig with everything you would normally take on a trip, including any passengers, and weigh the RV at a moving, coal, or trucking company or a state weighing station. You should also weigh each axle separately to see if you have properly distributed the weight. An overload will tax the safety capacity of the vehicle's suspension system. Read the owner's manual for the firm load limits and the suggestions on how to distribute the load.

Use the closets, cabinets, and drawers provided in your RV, but secure everything. Use paper towels, shock cord, items of clothing, and linens to make things snug. Avoid breakable pottery, glass dishes, and heavy metal. Be careful not to leave drawers, cabinet doors, or even the refrigerator door unlatched.

Do not place heavy objects at the rear of your vehicle. Keep trailer load weight near the axle, and truck camper load forward. The motor home has a front and a rear axle; keep the load midway between them. Keep the weight low. Secure heavy items so that they will not suddenly shift and upset the balance.

DRIVING

Driving an RV is not as difficult as it appears. Though they can be large, they are generally quite maneuverable after you become accustomed to the added length and weight. It is necessary to become thoroughly familiar with the rig's handling characteristics. They do take some initial getting used to and an increased level of skill, but these are easy to acquire.

The driver's seat of an RV places you higher than that of a regular car, giving added road visibility. Actually, this brings in an increased amount of enjoyment because you view the scenery from broader windows and a better (higher) perspective.

Develop some expertise in the following seven major areas peculiar to safe rig driving: stop/go, turning, clearance, tipping prevention, backing, hills, and repairs.

Stop/Go

All RVs take longer to stop or to accelerate. Because they cannot accelerate as fast as an automobile, you must make allowance for space when you merge onto an expressway; drive onto a busy highway from a side road; reenter a busy road from a roadside stop; make a left turn at an intersection; pass other vehicles.

Be aware of the distance needed to stop when braking. RVs cannot stop suddenly because of their additional weight. Learn to keep a safe distance between you and the vehicle ahead of you. With more distance you will have better visibility and can, for instance, see a stop sign ahead in time to slow down gradually. The formulas below will help you to judge the space needed to stop and to maintain a safe "space cushion" from the vehicle ahead.

To stop, allow one second for every ten feet of your vehicle length, always maintaining at least four seconds. Allow several extra seconds if the road is wet and slippery.

Maintain a safe distance from the vehicle ahead of you by allowing at least one length of the entire rig from front to back for every ten miles per hour that you are moving. A thirty-foot vehicle traveling at fifty miles per hour should allow 150 feet of space to the vehicle ahead.

Turning

Be careful when turning. The added height and weight of an RV make it susceptible to tipping over in a sudden turning movement.

The RV length requires a wider turn to stay in its own space. This means moving farther into the intersection before starting to turn. If you are pulling a trailer, turn from the center of the intersection into the right side of the lane and then bring your tow vehicle and the trailer into the center of it.

Use the hand-over-hand steering motion so that your rig is under tight control throughout the entire turning maneuver.

A curve on a highway needs to be negotiated with care. Take it slower than the suggested safe turning speed.

Clearance

Know the vehicle's clearance and watch for clearance height posted on most overhangs and underpasses. You will run into clearance restrictions at filling stations, shopping malls, motels, and tree branches on side roads. Most underpasses are high enough for passage. Learn to tell at a glance whether your vehicle will hit, but never take chances.

RVs usually have a higher ground clearance than automobiles. Inspect the underside, including the hitch, so you know exactly what you have. Driving a trailer over bumps and holes causes a downward thrust. Allow for this so you do not break a spring or an axle or the hitch.

Tipping Prevention

When a semitrailer, truck, or bus passes from behind, it may cause considerable turbulence around your rig. Check the mirrors for passing trucks. Then place your hands on the wheel in the ten o'clock and two o'clock positions and hold the steering wheel as steady as possible while the truck passes. Long trailers are more affected than shorter ones by the pull from passing trucks.

Being passed when you are not prepared for the suction causes the most trouble. If you are driving a motor home, take your foot off the gas and move as far to the right as the pavement will allow you to go, slowing your rig by five to ten miles per hour, no more. If you are driving a trailer, edge over in your lane as far as you safely can and accelerate slightly. Do not coast while the truck or bus passes you. If you are going downhill when the bus or truck passes you, gently apply the trailer brakes alone. If truck suction is a continuing problem, check your hitch equipment.

Strong winds that hit the rig broadside require attentive driving, because it will start swaying. Conventional trailers will sway more in high winds than motor homes and fifth wheel trailers. Decrease your speed, which gives the wheels a better grip on the pavement. When there are wind alerts, pull off the highway as far as possible, stop, and set the emergency brake. If the visibility is low and you are close to the road, turn off your lights so that other drivers will not be confused about the direction of the road.

Backing

Most drivers get help when backing an RV. If you do not have a TV installation monitored at the rear, develop a backing routine with a partner. Backing a motor home is easy once you get the hang of it, but backing a trailer is tricky.

Backing a trailer must be done slowly with small movements at the steering wheel. Stop and analyze what movement is needed before proceeding. It is not necessary to keep the rig moving all the time. If your trailer turns to a right angle to the hitch, all you can do is pull ahead and start over.

A trailer reacts opposite to the way the tow vehicle's wheels are turned. You will get a delayed interaction with the movement of the trailer, so go slowly. Once the trailer is in its turning mode, it will not continue in that direction. You will have to increase and decrease the rate of turn several times before the trailer is maneuvered into position.

Take your time. Stop frequently. Get out to look over the situation. Do not hesitate to pull forward as often as needed if the trailer starts to turn too much or you have misjudged the space. Avoid extremes in turning the wheel.

Hills

The weight of your rig will cause you to go uphill slowly. Be patient with this reduced speed and learn to live with it. Be careful of overheating going uphill in high altitude and hot weather.

Also, downshift when going downhill instead of constantly applying the brakes; they will overheat. Make it a practice to start down steep grades at a very slow speed to avoid heat buildup. Heated brakes require more pedal pressure and deplete reserve braking power. With a trailer, apply the trailer brakes to aid in slowing, but these should be activated only for a second or two and intermittently.

Be a courteous RV driver in situations when you are slower than the flow of traffic. Pull over to the side and let the cars behind you go by.

Repairs

The most common roadside breakdowns are flat tires and overheating.

If you have a flat tire, move the rig off the highway and to a safe place. Put out flares, flags, or reflective triangles and use flashers on the disabled vehicle or raise the hood and tie a white cloth to the antenna. If the rig is on a grade, put the transmission in park, set the parking brake, and place wedges against the wheels.

If the rig begins to overheat, try one of three different remedies: turn off the air conditioner; pull off the road and open the hood without touching the radiator cap, and put the engine in a fast idle to increase the air flow; or turn the heat all the way on and open the window (this helps to pump heat away from the engine).

Whether or not you do your own repairs, you should understand all the systems in your RV to make intelligent judgments about repair work. Instruction booklets are a good source of information. Look for RV manuals at libraries and bookstores. *Trailer Life* and *Motor Home* magazines have a regular feature of instructional articles about RV systems.

Here are your options if you need repairs while on the road:

• Call the manufacturer for advice. Look on the equipment's warranty or instruction booklet for a telephone number. Many have a toll-free number.

• Enroll in the Good Sam Emergency Road Service plan. This emergency service provides towing for all types of RV rigs. They can come to your disabled rig to make minor repairs or suggest garages that will make repairs at a fair price.

• Look for the American Automobile Association (AAA) Approved Repair Facilities, which are identified by a blue-and-white sign.

While your rig is being repaired, stay with it. The mechanic may allow you to be near and learn. You will be available for consultation and to check for honest work.

CHILDREN

Familiarize your children with the RV. This is a good time to set up standards or rules. For example, when showing them where things are kept in the refrigerator, emphasize the importance of firmly latching the door, sealing lids, and rewrapping neatly. Children, depending on the age, will want and need to know how to fold out the bed, manage the linens, clean up spills, and operate the sound systems.

There are times when the togetherness of RV living is more than the parent/child relationship can stand. Do not allow tensions to get out of control. The family vacation is a good time to put irritations on hold and build relationships.

MEALS

Take advantage of your RV conveniences. This is the perfect opportunity for quick, simple meals. Vacation is not the time to be complicated with fuss and mess in the kitchen. Spend your time on recreation, not housekeeping duties. The family will love a change of pace and different convenience-type treats not usually served at home. This is one of the big advantages over tent camping—you can use any of the convenience items in the grocery store because the cooking apparatus is at your fingertips.

Include appropriate kitchen gear for your RV. You will want pans that nest, unbreakable glasses and dishes, and appliances of your choice—toaster, can opener, popcorn popper, pancake grill.

You can find RV cookbooks at bookstores and RV supply stores. You might already have quick-meal cookbooks, and no doubt a cookbook with a chapter specializing on this style of cooking. Look them over. Personal preference is the key here.

CAMPSITE ARRIVAL AND DEPARTURE

Choose your site according to the size of your rig, accessibility, overhanging branches that interfere with parking, and level space. Ask about electrical and water hookups and a holding tank dump station.

Back into your camp. You never know when an emergency may necessitate a quick exit.

If the campsite provides only a 12-volt system and propane gas, be careful when turning on the gas. If you suspect a leak, check it by brushing a soapy solution on the questionable joints. Bubbles will appear if a leak exists. If you smell gas when entering an RV, never turn on or use anything that will cause an electrical spark or flame until you have opened all windows and doors, and the gas has dissipated. Check your propane cylinder on the first use of the season. If it contains air, it will have to be purged before being used.

When staying at campgrounds without electrical hookups, large-capacity batteries will allow you to live comfortably without a hookup. To get the best service from batteries, keep the terminals clean, and see that the battery water is at the proper level. A little petroleum jelly on the terminals helps prevent corrosion. Charge batteries that have been used for the night by running the engine of either a tow vehicle or motor home. Attach the connector cord between the trailer and the tow vehicle if you have that rig.

If your RV is new, or even second-hand, follow the manufacturer's instructions to sanitize the water tanks and lines.

Pulling out of the campsite is easy with an RV. Remember to prepare the rig for travel. Secure all that you have been using back into its original traveling position. Remember to secure cupboards, drawers, refrigerator doors, vehicle doors, windows, and vents. Turn off the lights and appliances and lock the outside door.

Take special precaution to close off any of the vehicle's apparatus that you are not familiar with. Turn off gas. Secure the LP (propane) bottles. Disconnect and store electrical, water, and sewer lines. Close the holding tank valve. Turn off the separate 12-volt system. Take down any window shield, awnings, and antennas.

RESOURCES

Wouldn't it be nice to have a listing of current publications (other than bookstore trade) about RVs? Write or call Recreation Vehicle

Industry Association, (main office) P.O. Box 2999, 1896 Preston White Drive, Reston, VA 22090 (1-707-620-6033); or (western office) 1748 West Katella Avenue, Suite 108, Orange, CA 92667 (1-714-532-1688) for the following information:

- RV shows
- RV rental sources
- Campground information
- State campground associations
- Camping clubs
- RV trade and related associations
- Publications for campers and RV owners
- RV accessibility for the handicapped
- RV trade publications
- Catalog of Publications about RV Lifestyle

Bookstores and libraries carry directories, which list RV campground accommodations. Look for the following publications: *Rand McNally RV Park and Campground Directory* (Rand McNally), *Trailer Life RV Campground & Services Directory* (TL Enterprises), *Wheelers Recreational Resort & Campground Guide* (Print Media Services), and *Woodell's Campground Directories* (Woodell Publishing Company).

5

Planning a Camping Trip

Successful camping trips begin long before you lock your door and drive away. There are a hundred details, some large and some small, that require your attention. Make the planning as much fun as the actual trip.

The first few trips require more planning than subsequent ones. It takes a little time to collect all the gear and establish your own routine. For this reason, many people first take some practice trips (shakedown trips) to established campgrounds close to home. Doing this with experienced campers for a short time such as a weekend is especially helpful. Let them know you are there to learn. If your two families are compatible, you may even decide you want to continue to camp with them. The fellowship on a camping trip is rewarding.

Remember that a practice trip does not give the full flavor of the fun because the purpose of it is more the practice than the fun. Also, some feel that weekend camping itself is a drawback. It is hard to set up camp for only two days. In some cases, it takes a few days to get into the routine of outdoor living and to get past any problems that might come up.

EXPENSES

As with any vacation, your financial resources need to be calculated when you consider taking a camping vacation. Expenses vary according to how many people go, where you go, and how long you are gone. Camping is economical, but it is not free. Every campground charges a fee for campsite use; this fee may range from a few dollars per night to as high as thirty dollars or so, depending on the amenities offered.

The only other expenses for a camping trip (assuming all equipment has been obtained) are mileage on your vehicle, gasoline, food, and personal items. Consider the following extras when you estimate the personal expenditures:

- Shopping
- Film
- Stamps and postcards
- Fishing licenses
- Souvenirs
- Ice cream cones
- Ice
- Allowances
- Soft drinks, coffee
- Sunscreen

- Fishing bait
- Rides
- Amusement
- Newspapers
- Magazines
- Firewood
- Laundry
- Showers
- Meals out
- Grocery store

Camping economics opens up a whole new world. You are now flexible: take off for weekends, visit relatives who live in a small house, view all places as a viable trip!

DESTINATION

When deciding where to go, first consider the distance. Calculate how much driving time is appropriate in proportion to the total vacation time, the comfort of your vehicle, and the individual differences of the passengers. Allow plenty of time for the road so that the driving can be part of the fun.

Within that distance range, narrow down the options to areas that offer what you like to do—mountain hiking, lake activities, seaside activities, sightseeing. Because camping is a pleasant, low-cost way to overnight for recreational activities, camp where your idea of the action is.

Researching a destination is where the fun begins. Look through the listings in the appendix for campsite opportunities in the areas that interest you. Write or call all of the districts in your target zone. When you receive information about an area, write or call for more details. For example, your first inquiry might be to the state parks office of a particular state. They will send you a list of the individual parks with campsites; then you can write or call one or more of the individual parks for specific information, such as the type of campsites there. This will help you decide if a campground offers what you are looking for.

You also might want to look into national campgrounds. The National Parks and Conservation Association is a wonderful source of this information. By joining the NPCA for $25 a year (memberships help preserve and protect our national parks), you get the *NPCA Regional Guide* to the national and state parks for your geographic region of the United States, a free subscription to the *National Parks* magazine, the NPCA "Park-Pak," which includes four national park publications, and a *Rand McNally Road Atlas & Travel Guide*. You also will be given access to a toll-free number for the parks' travel information, which gives basic information such as current weather conditions.

Your area utility company might provide recreation on the reservoirs and adjacent lands. Call to request information about camping opportunities. More resources are listed in the appendix.

As your begin to accumulate information on different camping areas, you will find that there are three basic types. The first, which can be called a completely pristine campsite, has not been used previously—at least not visibly. Advanced backpackers use these. No amenities are provided; there are no bathrooms, outhouses, firepits, or picnic tables. The campsite is usually very private and secluded.

The second type of campsite, which can be referred to as the rustic site, appeals to some advanced campers as well as some beginning campers. This camping-designated area does not have plumbing improvements (outhouses are used), but tent sites, firepits, and sometimes picnic tables are provided.

The campsites in an organized or established campground have a firepit, a picnic table, and community rest rooms, usually with hot water and showers. Sometimes organized campgrounds offer a variety of additional amenities, such as a grill stove, a latched cupboard, a public telephone, a ranger station with brochures and displays, marked trails, a beach, a boat launching site, and a large campfire area with seating that features campfire programs for the family. Some even take on the feeling of a resort, with a swimming pool, a recreation hall, a tennis court, and more. They charge a higher campsite fee than more simple campgrounds.

The material you receive when you write for information will acquaint you with what's available so you can narrow down your list of preferences. You may discover that one campground does not permit campfires, so you decide not to go there. If you are thinking about taking a pet with you, you will find your choices are greatly limited, as most campgrounds prohibit pets.

Then, in order to make a final selection, you may want to research the recreation opportunities offered in the vicinity of the different campgrounds. You will find listings of these resources in the appendix. For example, each state office of tourism puts together a packet of information. Some packets include maps, camping brochures, specific activities for the year, and information about the state. Usually there is a colorful, glossy magazine with special features and pertinent facts. Do not miss out on this resource.

The U.S. Fish & Wild Life Service offers recreation opportunities such as observation towers, auto tour routes, hiking trails, and species to photograph at its various refuge sites. You might find there is one near your campsite. Write them for a very nice, glossy, colored U.S. map with a chart on the back designating all of the visitor opportunities at specific refuges.

With so many resources available, planning will be a recreation in itself. Allow enough time to savor this aspect. Before tucking pertinent information in your camp travel file, keep the materials that you collect in a central location of the house. Let the family browse through them to stimulate their interest and serve as an impetus for further research.

The final step in this part of the planning procedure is to think about the best time to go. Consider the possible weather conditions, how crowded a campground might be, and the timing of recreational opportunities between May and September—the high season of camping. The chamber of commerce in your chosen area will be the best source of this information.

MAKING RESERVATIONS

The reservation procedure varies from one type of campground to another. The information you received will be your source of instructions.

To reserve a campsite in a national park, make your reservation through a Ticketron agency. Ticketron is listed in your local telephone book. Call them way in advance to find out the location of the Ticketron office in your area. You can make reservations eight weeks in advance. Ask them how fast your choice fills up. They only accept cash. The reservation form explains two other ways to make reservations.

GETTING READY TO GO

You are ready for the trip-planning procedure when you have made your reservations.

An important highlight of planning a family camping vacation is holding a family meeting to discuss it. Remember that you want to enlist the children's input and participation in order to make the trip successful for everyone. Seize this family meeting opportunity for communication. Listen for:

- Expectations
- General input
- Venting

- Clothing needs
- Itinerary preferences
- Menu suggestions
- Responses to the division of responsibilities
- Offers to take on projects (research, food preparation, log book)

Start organizing your family for the vacation early on when you are not in a hurry or under the pressure of a deadline. Develop a note-taking system for jotting down all thoughts that come to you. Start with:

- Gear to bring
- Food to buy and take (some food can be bought near the campground)
- Food to freeze
- Small items to buy or set aside (such as sewing kit, games, can opener, whisk broom)
- Calls to make
- Questions to ask
- Details for closing off the house
- Medical checkups
- CPR classes
- Clothing to set aside
- Clothing to buy
- Haircuts
- Car maintenance
- Cut toenails to prevent infection

Prepare yourself for a little hiking and/or swimming. You can do some stretches and take some walks with a good stride to prepare your body for the extra physical exercise that is coming.

A few days before leaving, call the campground with any last-minute questions. You might ask how far the nearest rural grocery or supermarket is, or how the weather has been and how it looks for the next few days.

PACKING

Pack your gear from a list. Use it as a checklist to guide you through the packing details and to remind you of what must be done at the last minute. Be selective about what you lug along.

Pack clothes in large plastic bags (preferably with a drawstring), pillow cases tied at the top with ribbon or string, or duffel bags. These can be squeezed between other items. Take a few extra bags and, when packing up to come home, sort the laundry for washing at home. Take a suitcase of apparel for special occasions—church, special restaurants, and visiting. This will keep clothing items clean and nice until needed.

Stuff sleeping bags into their stuff sack. Most of the gear should be in its original box for traveling and storage.

Gather everything you are taking in a large room and arrange in categories—clothing, sleeping items, kitchen equipment, campsite gear, accessible travel items, handy travel items—to get a visual image of what is going. (You can line up the bulky outdoor items on a convenient patio or driveway spot so that they are visible and categorized.) Organize all food, except the ice chest items, right along with the rest of the piles. (You might want to put the ice chest out where you can see it to plan on keeping a space for it in the car.)

Now, take a good look at everything; think it through, check what you see against your list. Set aside the items that need to be accessible and those that need to be very handy. Load the items not according to categories but according to size and weight. When loading, balance the weight and keep in mind the principle—last in, first out. Remember to pack the car tools where they can be easily reached. Just before you leave, fill the ice chest and load it into the car.

6

At the Campground

Turning into the campground is a big moment. Plan to arrive during daylight hours, allowing several hours to put up the tent, unpack, and set things up. You can arrive anytime after the check-in time, which is usually in the early afternoon.

Most campgrounds have an office or ranger station for checking-in purposes. Usually they will assign a campsite to you, but if you have a special request, now is the time to speak up. You might want to ask to be near the rest room or water tap, set back from the road, in a sunny spot, or in a shady spot. If you have children, consider safety. Some sites may be next to a creek. If you are likely to spend all your time at the campsite worrying about your children falling into the creek, then choose another spot.

Once you have checked in, you will be given a permit. Campgrounds usually want it displayed on your windshield or dashboard as you drive in and out.

SETTING UP CAMP

Everyone helps unload the car. Stack everything on the picnic table. Assign the children to some tasks that are helpful and enjoyable.

If you are camping at high altitudes, take it easy. Your heart is working overtime.

Putting up the Tent

Setting up the tent is something the whole family can do together. The children will learn how to do the job and also can be a big help.

A typical campsite

If they are old enough for an auxiliary tent, they will enjoy putting it up.

Before setting up the tent, watch out for anthills, beehives, hornets' nests, and a concentration of ants on hanging limbs. Check the slope of the ground. Most established campsites are fairly flat, have good drainage, and are located away from water runoff. Find a spot where the tent will be able to face southeast, so it gets morning sun but is apt to be in the shade during the warm afternoon. (Use your compass, if necessary.) If possible, try to position the tent so it is not too close to the firepit. You do not want sparks from a fire to land on the tent and burn a hole in the fabric. Also, if you have a young child who goes to bed early, while the rest of the family sits around the campfire, he will be kept awake by your voices if he is too nearby. If the tent is located too close to the firepit and kitchen working area, your late-morning sleepers may be disturbed while you prepare breakfast.

Clear away rocks or other obstructions from your chosen tent site, but leave the humus there. Spread out the ground cloth and set up the tent. Tuck in the ground cloth so that there is no protrusion. If it rains, the water would collect there. Put a small, washable rug or a straw mat in front of the tent to keep the inside and the bedding clean.

Setting up the Kitchen

Organize your kitchen so it is convenient for you. Put the cooler chest in the shade. Set up an auxiliary table for the camp stove, utensils, pans, and cooking supplies. Use another end of another table for tableware, food, and paper supplies. Another small auxiliary table can be set up for dishwashing with dishpans, soap, scouring pads, sponge, paper towels, and chlorine bleach. (You can sterilize your camp dishes by adding a little bit of chlorine bleach—one teaspoon to a gallon of water—to the final rinse water. (Do not rinse steel, aluminum, silver, or chipped enamel in this solution.)

Remember to keep fuel canisters away from the stove and the firepit. This is important and worth repeating—keep fuel canisters away from the stove and the firepit.

Set up your garbage bag. If you are using a plastic bag, it can be tied around a tree with a piece of rope or a bungie cord, leaving an opening in the bag for filling it. A paper grocery bag with a rock in the bottom to prevent it from blowing away also is useful and can be placed right next to your working area for easy accessibility.

If you are going to eat on T.V. tables around the fire, keep the table provided by the campground clear for games, reading, and writing.

Fill your folding water container at a nearby water tap. Set it on your work table.

Setting up Small Items

The following suggestions are important for camp comfort. If you have brought a dining canopy (fly) install it above the table. Follow the manufacturer's directions to set it up with its poles or with ropes tied to tree branches.

Install a clothesline. Secure the rope to branches or around trunks of surrounding trees. (Never nail anything onto a tree in a camping area.) Position the clothesline for providing clothesline space and privacy, but remember that it is dangerous at neck height.

Set up the hammock. A hammock is easy to install, but you need to find two trees at the right distance. Be careful that the ropes cannot cause injuries at night, and instruct your children about using it safely and calmly. The hammock provides a place for fun and relaxation right at your campsite.

Your lantern can be hung from a rope or left on a table and moved around as needed.

Get firewood. If you are not allowed to gather firewood, purchase some at the ranger station in time for your evening campfire.

THE CAMPFIRE

If there is one traditional symbol of camping, it is the campfire. A campfire represents fellowship, romance, nostalgia, daydreams, relaxation, warmth, and food.

Reading aloud by the campfire sets an atmosphere of togetherness as well as relaxation. You might try a combination of inspirational and entertaining selections. If your group likes to sing, get it together with *Campfire Songs* by Irene Maddox (Globe Pequot).

Always remember to watch children around the fire. Never put empty fuel canisters in the firepit.

Building a Fire

Fire making is a skill. When you understand the principles, you can build a roaring fire.

Light the fire at the bottom of the tinder. Always light the fire upwind, that is with the wind blowing directly to the match.

There are three fire styles, which you can make in this order, all on the same fire. For a teepee fire, stack kindling (twigs, small

The campfire

branches, well-split logs) over the tinder (paper, leaves, twigs) so that it is arranged in a circle and leans together at the top for support, forming a teepee. When the basic teepee has burned, it will leave a good bed of coals for the remainder of wood, which can be laid flat. Now take your heavy firewood (logs, split if very large), setting aside the biggest three or four for the next step. Begin with the biggest and lay them flat, forming a square in crisscross fashion that resembles a log-cabin construction. Let this burn for a while and lay the largest logs, which you set aside, around in a circle with one end pointing in the fire and with the tips stacked on each other a little to form a star fire. As the tips burn, shove them into the fire.

Homemade Fire Starters

If you think you are going to have any difficulty finding dry leaves or twigs around your campsite to help get your fire started, make some fire starters at home with the family before your trip. They never fail.

FIRE STARTER NO. 1. - Cut about four or five sheets of newspaper into strips that are five inches wide. Roll the strips up moderately tight and tie a string around each one. Using a can in a frying pan of boiling water, melt candle stumps or paraffin wax that is sold in block form for canning. Do not overheat the wax. It should be just hot enough to melt. Drop in the paper rolls. Remove after thirty seconds or when they are coated with wax. Lay them out to cool.

FIRE STARTER NO. 2. - Fill cardboard egg carton cups with lint from your dryer or with shredded paper. Fill each cup half full of melted wax. Break off the desired amount as you use them.

FIRE STARTER NO. 3. - Take along a bag of cotton balls and a big jar or tube of petroleum jelly. When you want a fire starter, just dip the balls into the jelly or smear it on and toss them into the fire.

CAMPGROUND ETIQUETTE

Campers share the same territory, so group cooperation is essential.

- Do not cut across anyone's campsite
- Do not pollute streams or lake water
- Do not clean fish, wash clothes or dishes, or spit toothpaste into the water
- Do not feed wildlife (it destroys their ability to fend for themselves)
- Be quiet at night and in the early morning hours
- Keep the restrooms clean
- Do not cut or pick flowers and do not mutilate trees or shrubs
- Do not chop or pull down a bough of a tree
- Leave your campsite clean
- Do not litter; all garbage goes in a garbage can no matter how far away one is
- Stay on paths

PROPERTY PROTECTION

There is some theft in campgrounds. It is wise to develop a camping style that cuts down the risk of being a victim.

- Keep valuables and nice things locked up or out of sight
- Expensive-looking gear attracts attention
- Even an expensive car attracts thievery
- While airing sleeping bags, do not leave the campsite
- Do not look for suspicious people because the professionals are indistinguishable from real campers

A TYPICAL DAY

Two words—flexible and fun—describe the typical camping day.

The Morning

There is no need to rush to get up on a camping morning. You may be awakened early by the sound of birds singing and by the sunlight on your tent, but you can stay warm and snug in your sleeping bag as long as you like.

If you do arise early, keep your voice down to almost a whisper. Remind your children about this. It is rude to wake up other campers in the morning. You will probably want to get dressed for breakfast before leaving your tent, using the layering system according to the weather.

If the morning is chilly, heating water for cocoa and coffee probably will be your first activity and building a fire in the firepit your second. Prepare breakfast at your leisure, taking time to enjoy the aroma of food cooking, the sound of the crackling fire, and the fresh air. Pull your camp chair up to the campfire to enjoy its warmth while you eat your breakfast at your T.V. table, and savor the luxury of lingering over your meal.

If you have not already formulated your day's plans, do so now, while everyone is relaxed and comfortable. Is this a day to relax around the campsite, take a hike or a bicycle ride, go fishing in a nearby lake, or go sightseeing? Your plans will help you determine whether you will have lunch at the campsite, pack a picnic, or buy it.

Heat water for dishwashing in your large kettle on the campfire, saving camp stove fuel. (If the firepit does not come with a grill on which you can put the kettle, put a rock in the middle of the campfire and set the kettle on it. Note: Any pot used over the fire will blacken with soot. You can wipe it off fairly easily if you have coated the pot exterior with liquid detergent before use. Otherwise, let the pot stay black and keep it specifically for this use.) While someone washes the breakfast dishes, another person can pack up the day's snacks and lunch. Maybe you will start a pit-cooked dinner. Clean up your kitchen area and wipe crumbs off the tables to keep from attracting insects. Seal boxes and bags of food and put them away where ground squirrels and chipmunks will not get into them during the day. Get rid of your garbage in the campground's garbage container.

Enlist your children's help in tidying up the tent. It is a good idea to air out the sleeping bags for a few hours during the day by draping them over a shaded clothesline. This dries out the body moisture from the night. Open the tent windows to air out the tent, but be sure to leave the tent door zipped tight to keep out insects. Sweep the tent with your whisk broom. Shake out the rug or mat. Pick up your gear and belongings from the campsite. Campers are neat and do not strew items around.

Before leaving the campsite for the day, put the campfire out according to campground rules. Snug your tent, closing the windows and putting on the tent fly, in case of a sudden storm.

Taking a Shower

A number of established campgrounds have hot showers. Some of them charge for a shower, which may be on a timer; be sure to take the right change and enough of it. You will quickly learn the best time to take a shower to avoid waiting in line; usually the showers are busiest between nine and ten o'clock in the morning and four and five o'clock in the afternoon.

Keep this refreshing time from being a hassle by working out a system. A couple of shower totes per person are handy; plastic bags with handles work fine. Use one for an outfit change and the other for towel, washcloth, soap, and toiletries. Use a second towel of a different color for a floor mat while you dress. Wear shower shoes if you like.

These rest rooms are likely to have electric outlets if you want to use a hairdryer or electric razor.

Hang your towels and washcloth on the clothesline back at the campsite and put soiled clothes in their proper place.

The Evening

Toward evening the campground starts bustling again as satisfied, happy families return from a full day of activities. Dinner preparations begin. If it is a chilly evening, this is the time to start the fire in the firepit. Everyone can help with dinner preparation. Get water, set the picnic table or the T.V. tables by the fire, and arrange serving spoons and condiments so they are accessible. Just before starting to eat, start heating the kettle of water on the fire for the dinner dishes.

Light the lantern when it starts getting dark out. Do your dishes before it is fully dark, if possible, so you can see what you are doing. The mosquitos might be getting bad around now, so put on some insect repellent. Bring your flashlights out to the table where you can find them easily.

Besides enjoying your campfire during the evenings, do plan to take advantage of the excellent evening programs provided by the

An evening campfire program taught by ranger/naturalist

state and national parks. The entire family can join in singing, skits, and educational presentations about the area.

78

Remember to keep the noise down during the evening when some campers are trying to sleep. Evening activities of song, merriment, and bedtime routine with children can get loud. Some campgrounds regulate a quiet time between certain hours, such as ten or eleven o'clock and dawn.

Everyone seems to have a different idea on what to wear to bed when camping. If you are camping in the mountains, it will be cold in the evening and in the morning, even if it is hot in the afternoon. Use the layering principle, which involves wearing a number of complementary, lightweight garments, rather than one or two bulky ones. In the evening, before or after dinner, dress in the layers needed from the underwear layer out, adding as the evening grows colder. When you slip into your sleeping bag, shed to the long underwear. In the chilly morning, you will be glad to leave that first layer on, slipping your clothes on over it. Remember to wear a hat to bed on cold nights. Using the layering principle varies with the seasons; apply it to suit your needs.

Spend the last few minutes before bed revitalizing your body with plenty of heat for the night. Exercise mildly to speed up your metabolism. Take a brisk walk around the campground or to a scenic spot. Warm up by the campfire. Enjoy the drowsy feeling that comes with the heat and the relaxation. Eat some food that is high in carbohydrates; it will increase your natural blood sugar and create heat in your body. Hot chocolate is perfect. (Rinse off your dirty dishes before going to bed so they do not attract animals. You can give them a good washing in the morning.)

Just before retiring, store all food (except unopened cans or jars), the ice chest, and the garbage in your car with the windows up. Some campsites have a latched cabinet where food is safe from animals at night. Bears and raccoons are attracted by the odor of food. If a bear smells something it wants, it can even tear open an ice chest for it. Do not keep food in your tent unless you want to wake up to furry visitors.

Finally, check the campground rule about the campfire.

Although some allow the fire to die on its own during the night, you would want to be very sure that there is no chance of the night getting windy and sparks being blown from the firepit. If the campground says the fire must be totally extinguished, douse it with water, poke around in the coals, and douse some more.

A RAINY DAY

If rain is predicted, especially a heavy rain, prepare for it. Be certain the tent rainfly is on taut. Some have additional loops at the bottom so they can be staked away from the tent to give good ventilation; you do not want the fly to cling to the tent. If the rain is going to be heavy, dig a small canal around your tent to channel rainwater away from it (be sure to fill up the canal before you leave).

Get everyone in their rain gear and encourage them to stay dry. Do not allow wet clothes inside the tent because the moisture will evaporate into the tent air and condense on clothing and bedding.

If you are going to stay at the campsite during the rain, find activities to do at the picnic table under the dining canopy. This is a wonderful time for the family to play a favorite board or card game. You also can work on a puzzle together, read, or tell stories. If you want to go somewhere, you may be able to find a nearby bowling alley, movie theater, roller skating rink, local industry or plant tour, or museum. There is no reason why you should let the rain ruin your camping trip—it just gives you an opportunity to find a different sort of recreation for a while.

7

Camping Food

Meals are an important part of any holiday. But when camping, the emphasis must be tempered with simplicity. It is essential that no undue strain be put on the cook. Make sure that everyone knows they are going to help. Children will be willing when they pick up on the festive atmosphere. Enjoy easy meals and keep in mind an old saying, "The lazy camper has the most fun."

DO-AHEAD FOOD PLANNING

Even if convenience foods are not your everyday style, take advantage of them when camping. Look for condensed, dehydrated, canned, and dried foods. Tasty advancements have been made in soups, drink mixes, cereals, and snack foods—all friends of the vacation cook. If you prefer natural foods with whole grains and fewer desserts, you will find products you can use—crackers, applesauce, beverages, and much more. Remember the foods that are *naturally* convenient: all dried fruit, apples, oranges, and unshelled peanuts.

If you enjoy ham, a canned ham is always useful on a camping trip. It is handy, tasty, and versatile. Buy one from the shelf, not the refrigerator section, so you can pack it with the dry food. If you do buy a refrigerated canned ham, it is best to store it in the ice chest.

There are certain basic pantry items that come in handy for cooking and snacks while camping. They are:

- Salt and pepper
- Granulated sugar
- Brown sugar
- Powdered sugar
- Honey
- Biscuit mix

- Cocoa mix
- Powdered milk
- Coffee, tea
- Powdered juice drink
- Vegetable oil
- Jam and/or jelly
- Marshmallows
- Popcorn (popcorn poppers sold at camping supply stores)

- Peanuts in shell
- Dried fruits
- Peanut butter
- Graham crackers
- Snack and/or soda crackers
- Beef jerky
- Dry soup(s)

Plan your meals in advance, to be certain that you take everything you will need. Will you be making pancakes one morning? Think about what you will need to make them and what your family likes to put on them. Instead of taking a large container of maple syrup, which takes up a lot of space, you might want to pack a small one. Think through your usual sandwich-making procedure. Will you need mayonnaise for someone's sandwich? If you can take a small jar instead of a large one, do so, as it will take up less space in your ice chest. How much margarine or butter should you have? Will it be used on sandwiches, bread, and pancakes, in the pan for cooking the pancakes and frying eggs, and mixed in with a bowlful of popcorn? Bring enough for all needs.

Have you thought about snacks suitable for all ages? Some good camping snacks are individual boxes of juice, carrot sticks, celery sticks, raisins, corn chips, crackers, cheese, quartered peanut butter sandwiches, and popcorn. Just be careful about giving some of these to young children. Carrots, popcorn, and nuts, as well as hard candies may make a young child choke.

The purpose in thinking through all your meals and the foods you will be using is to prevent you from forgetting or running out of something and needing to go shopping. This is your vacation!

After you have planned your meals and snacks, write your grocery list. Consider dividing the list so that you buy some things at a supermarket near your destination and take some things from home. There are tradeoffs in managing your shopping list this way. Consider the length of travel (because time wears down on the life of the ice in the ice chest), the amount of space you can spare for food, the possibility of higher prices at the destination end (if a supermarket is not near the campground), the additional fuel expense due to the heavier travel load, and personal convenience. A good compromise is to plan on stopping at a supermarket in the town next to your campground. There the prices will not be as high as at the smaller country stores, and even if you planned on bringing everything from home, you will think of something that sounds good or that you forgot. You might want to buy some milk, a little meat, some fresh fruit, and some new ice, as well as any heavy items like a gallon of juice.

Freezing and Cooling Foods

Your ice chest will stay colder longer if you start out with contents that are as cold as possible. Items that can be frozen ahead of time and then stored in the ice chest before you leave include: meat, cheese, juices in cardboard containers, and water. Fill the plastic screw-in containers that come with your ice chest with water and freeze them in advance. Use clean water and clean containers so that you can drink this water if desired. Or, freeze water in milk cartons.

The ice chest will need new ice about every two to four days. Purchase ice at the local store. In determining how long you can keep perishables, such as meat, dairy products, and mayonnaise, figure that a camp ice chest is slightly less efficient than the refrigerator. For maximum efficiency, open the ice chest as little as possible, keep it covered, and place it in the shade.

DO-AHEAD FOOD PREPARATION

One way to simplify meal preparation at the campground is to prepare some foods ahead of time and take them with you. Bread and desserts are two good things to take, ready to enjoy at any time.

Making dried foods gives you a head start on wilderness trips and backpacking, because these foods are lightweight and keep well.

Baking

Sometimes it is nice to have some special "camping only" recipes. Make them a family tradition. Bake them at home and bring them along; you will be glad to have them on your vacation.

Mount Logan Bread

Here is a classic for the wilderness, and it keeps well too.

3 cups flour (white and/or whole wheat)

3/4 cup wheat germ

1/4 cup brown sugar

1/2 cup powdered milk

1/2 to 1 cup shelled nuts (walnuts, pecans, cashews, peanuts)

1/2 cup raisins

1/2 cup chopped dried fruit (peaches, apricots, dates, apples)

2 tablespoons peanut oil

1 cup honey

6 eggs

1. Mix flour, wheat germ, brown sugar, powdered milk, nuts, raisins, and dried fruit. Stir in peanut oil, honey, and eggs. Mixture should be heavier than quick-bread dough.

2. Spray a 9 x 5 1/4 x 2 3/4-inch bread pan with a nonstick coating. Pour in the batter and tap the pan on the counter. Press the batter down lightly. Bake in a preheated 275-degree oven for 2 hours. Cool 10 minutes before taking out of pan.

Yield: 18 slices

Backpacker's Superbars

This one is a winner. Make a lot; they are yummy. The *whole* almonds and the orange rind are unusual additions to bar cookies. The topping is firm enough for packing.

1/2 cup margarine

3/4 cup packed brown sugar

1/2 cup quick-cooking oats

1 cup white flour (or 1/2 cup white, 1/2 cup whole wheat)

1/4 cup toasted wheat germ (or a nutty cereal ground in blender)

2 teaspoons grated orange rind

2 eggs

1 cup whole almonds (blanched, natural, or toasted)

1/4 cup raisins

1/4 cup flaked coconut

1/2 cup semisweet chocolate chips

1. Beat together the margarine and 1/2 cup of the brown sugar. Add oats, flour, wheat germ, and orange rind and mix. Pat this mixture into an ungreased 8-inch square pan.

2. Using the same bowl, mix eggs, almonds, raisins, coconut, chocolate chips, and remaining 1/4 cup brown sugar. Pour this mixture over the base and spread evenly. Bake in a preheated 350-degree oven for about 30 to 35 minutes. Cool before cutting.

Yield: 12 squares

Food Drying

If you will be doing any backpacking, you might want to invest in a food dehydrator. If you do not have a dehydrator, you can do some food drying in a slow oven or microwave.

Oven drying is done at a very low heat. You want the air around the food to absorb the moisture and carry it away. Avoid trapping the moisture in the oven. If your oven door is tight fitting, prop the door open about a half inch. Sometimes you can see steam escaping from the food, especially during the initial stages of cooking. All recipes are done when the moisture is completely cooked out; they usually are a little crisp at this point. Burning is a definite hazard during the final stages of cooking, so be very careful to stir frequently and stand by.

When drying in a microwave oven, use a low setting. The temperature at this setting varies a little with different oven models, so you may need to take a little time at first to find the proper setting for your microwave. Microwave drying needs more frequent checks during the final stages than a conventional oven does. Always stand by and reposition the food, remembering that the food in the center cooks more slowly than the edges.

Dried food will keep for at least a month in a covered container or plastic bag when placed in a cool, dry area. Always cool the food thoroughly before packaging.

Tomato Leather

This may come out of the oven looking like leather; however, do not be dismayed if yours comes out in pieces. It is just as good and useful. Use it as a cooking ingredient with water whenever you need tomato sauce, tomato paste, or tomato juice.

1–3 8-ounce cans tomato puree

1. For oven drying, use up to 3 cans of puree per 11 x 17-inch jelly-roll pan. Spray the pan with a nonstick coating and spread out the puree evenly. Set in a 150-degree oven for about 10 hours. Turn it over after 8 or 9 hours.

2. For microwave drying, spray a microwave-proof low-edged pan

with nonstick coating. Spread 1 can of puree evenly in the pan. Cook on low power for about 60 to 70 minutes. Every 15 minutes redistribute the center portion to the outer edges, keeping the bottom of the pan scraped.

3. Near the end of the drying time, watch carefully that the tomato leather does not burn. It is done when it is crisp and thoroughly dry. Remove from the pan with a spatula and cool completely before putting in a container.

Yield: 11/2 to 2 cups oven-dried leather and 1/2 cup microwave dried.

Dried Cottage Cheese Flakes

This is wonderful when soaked in a little water for a few minutes to go back to its soft consistency. It also is good plain, as a fruit topping and on top of spaghetti, pizza, chili, stew, and soup. It turns out a little browned in the microwave and pure white in the oven.

1/2–1 cup low-fat cottage cheese, large or small curd

1. For oven drying, spray a 10 x 15-inch jellyroll pan with a nonstick coating. Evenly spread 1 cup cottage cheese in the pan. Bake in a 150-degree oven for about 5 1/2 hours. Stir with a spatula, loosening the bottom as necessary, during the last half hour.

2. For microwave drying, spread 1/2 cup cottage cheese evenly over a flat-surfaced microwave-proof cooking dish. Cook for about 20 minutes at low setting. Toward the end of cooking, scrape it from the bottom of the pan.

3. Near the end of the cooking time, watch very carefully that the cottage cheese does not burn. It is done when it is crisp. Remove with a spatula, let cool completely and package.

Yield: 1/2–3/4 cup oven-dried flakes, 1/4 cup microwave-dried flakes

Dried Crumbled Meat

Use as you would hamburger in spaghetti, pizza, rice, chili, soup, or any casserole.

about 1/4 pound trimmed, cut-up, raw beef
1/4 cup soy sauce
about 1 1/4 cups water

1. Marinate beef in soy sauce for about 15 minutes. Drain and discard soy sauce. Cook in a pressure cooker or microwave oven with the water until tender.

2. Puree the meat and 1/4 cup of the liquid in a blender.

3. For oven drying, spray an 11 x 17-inch jellyroll pan with a nonstick coating. Spread the pureed meat evenly on the pan. Cook in a 150-degree oven for about 4 hours. Stir occasionally during the last hour. Watch carefully to prevent burning.

4. For microwave drying, spray a flat microwave-proof dish with a nonstick coating. A 9 x 9-inch glass baking dish also will work. Spread the pureed meat in the pan. Cook at a low setting for 30 minutes. Stir after 15 minutes and then watch carefully so that it does not burn.

5. It is done when it is crisp.

Yield: 3/4 cup crumbled meat

Beef Jerky

Here is a classic camper's snack.

1/2 to 1 pound roast or steak, 1/2 to 1 inch thick
1/2 cup soy sauce

1. Slice beef with the grain into strips as thin as possible. Marinate in the soy sauce up to 1 hour.

2. For oven drying, lay strips on a cookie rack placed on an 11x17-inch jellyroll pan. Cook in a 150-degree oven for 8 to 9 hours. Watch for burning during the last hour.

3. For microwave drying, lay 8 strips on a ridged microwave pan that is designed for bacon and other meat. Cook on low heat for 45 minutes. Watch for burning during the last 10 minutes.

4. They are done when they are crisp.

Yield: about 8–16 strips

Granola

Use this as a cold cereal and also a gorp snack.

4 cups rolled oats, instant or regular
2 cups shredded coconut
1 cup sesame seeds
1 cup chopped almonds
1 cup chopped cashews
1 cup safflower oil
1 cup honey
1 tablespoon vanilla
1/4 to 1/2 cup brown sugar
1/4 teaspoon salt
1 cup raisins
1 cup chopped or snipped dried apricots
1 cup chopped or snipped prunes

1. Combine the oats, coconut, sesame seeds, and nuts in a large bowl.

2. Heat the oil, honey, vanilla, brown sugar, and salt in a saucepan. Add them to the bowl of dry ingredients and mix well.

3. Spray a large (13 x 19-inch) sheet pan with a nonstick coating.

Evenly spread the ingredients in the pan. Bake in a 250-degree oven for about 50 minutes. Stir with a spatula every 15 minutes and then every 5 minutes near the end of cooking. You want it lightly browned, but you want to be careful that it does not burn. (It will turn crisp after it cools.)

4. After baking, cool slightly, then add the dried fruit. Cool completely and store in an airtight container.

Yield: 14 cups

Noncook Snacks

Gorp

Here is a hiker's standby. Some say it stands for "Good Old Raisins and Peanuts." Gorp is basically a mixture of fruit and nuts, and some people add candies. Do your own thing.

1 cup peanuts
1 cup raisins
1 cup chocolate-covered candies
Coconut flakes, butterscotch chips, and/or almonds (optional)

Mix all ingredients well. Store in an airtight container.

Yield: 3 or more cups

HOT-ASH OR FOIL COOKING

Using the right kind of coals is the most important factor when cooking in foil. A blazing fire will not do, so start your fire well ahead of cooking time to allow it to die down to glowing embers. Charcoal can be used as a base to get good coals easily. Hot coals alone are too hot. Mix them with ashes to temper the heat.

Spread out two or three thicknesses of foil (heavy-duty foil if you have it). Literally coat the top surface with margarine, butter, or oil to prevent the food from sticking to it. Place your food on the foil and wrap carefully. Seal (crimp) the edges securely. Make a second wrap that covers the seal with a smooth covering. Shovel the coals aside; lay the foil-wrapped food to be cooked on the hot ashes and cover it with ashes and coals. After the food has cooked the recommended time, have some kitchen tongs and heavy gloves available for picking the packages off the coals. Be careful of the escaping steam when you open the package.

Broasted Corn

1 ear corn per person
Salt to taste
Butter or mayonnaise to taste

Carefully pull back (but do not pull off) husk and remove silk by washing. Sprinkle with salt and dab with butter or mayonnaise on wet corn; replace husk, wrap in foil. Cook in hot ashes for 15 to 20 minutes, turning every 3 to 5 minutes.

Potatoes

1 baking potato per person
1 large onion, sliced
Butter to taste
Salt and pepper to taste
Seasonings (optional)

Scrub potatoes and slice into 3/4-inch slices. Place a very thin slice of onion between every third potato slice. Dab with butter between the slices, and sprinkle with salt, pepper, and additional seasoning to taste. Wrap each potato firmly in foil. Cook in hot ashes about 1 hour.

Baked Apple

1 apple per person
1 tablespoon brown or white sugar per apple

Wash apple. Cut a slice off the top, remove the core, and put the sugar in the hollow. Wrap in foil. Cook in hot ashes about 1 hour.

Camp Bread

2 cups biscuit mix
1/2 cup plus 1 tablespoon milk

1. Stir the ingredients together; this will make a very thick dough. Add a few teaspoons of milk if necessary. Shape it like a bread loaf, and dust with additional biscuit mix or flour.

2. Grease a large sheet of foil heavily. Place the dough on the foil and wrap it loosely so the foil package will not burst when the dough rises. Wrap the dough loosely again to cover the seams and crimping.

3. Place the bread package at the edge of the coals and turn every 10 minutes for about 1 1/2 hours, depending on the intensity of the heat.

Yield: 1 loaf

Complete Meal

Meat, seasoned to taste
Potatoes
Other vegetables

Cut meat, potatoes, and other vegetables into bite-size pieces. Divide the ingredients into individual portions on pieces of foil. Wrap each portion carefully. Cook in hot ashes about 1 to 2 hours. Serve in foil.

Mountain Melts

Rolls (any kind)
Cheese (sliced)
Meat (thinly sliced)
Mustard

Cut and butter rolls. Fill to taste with cheese, meat, and mustard.
Wrap each roll in foil. Place rolls on the edge of the coals or on grill
above the coals for about 1/2 to 1 hour.

OPEN-FIRE COOKING

Sit around the campfire; stay warm and cook some food on a stick.
This is a wonderful aspect of camping. Use a green, straight stick that
is about as big around as your thumb, or a cooking fork or straight-
ened-out wire hanger. These sticks should be brought as gear; you
should not pick them at a campground. Peel the sticks at the cooking
end. You can use it to cook a hot dog over the fire or a piece of bread
for your breakfast toast.

You can cook these recipes with some flame, but it is best when
some coals have formed.

Mock Coconut Angel Cake

6 thick (3/4- to 1-inch) slices bread
14 ounces sweetened condensed milk (make your own with equal
portions milk, powdered milk, and powdered sugar)
1 cup shredded coconut

Cut bread slices into fourths. Dip the squares in the milk, then roll in
the shredded coconut. Pierce the prepared square with a two-
pronged fork and toast over the fire coals until lightly browned.
Reverse position of the bread to brown both sides. Be careful, as this
burns easily.

Yield: 24 squares

Crescent Rolls on a Stick

These take a little time and patience. It is a good evening activity with fellowship and singing. The dough must bake without burning.

Crescent rolls sold in tubes
Butter or margarine
Jam, jelly, or honey

1. Using a thick stick about 1 1/2 inches in diameter, wrap the dough for one crescent roll spiral fashion around the tip of the stick. Allow enough space within the spiral for the heat to reach all of the dough. Press just the ends of the dough to the stick so that it will adhere during baking but slip off when done.

2. Hold the stick over the coals for 15 to 20 minutes, turning frequently, until the crescent roll is golden brown. Slip it off the stick, spread with butter and fill with jam, jelly, or honey.

Yield: 1–3 rolls per person suggested

Barbecue

Barbecuing is perfect for camp cooking. Campsites sometimes have barbecue grills. You might want to bring the grill from home, however, because camp grills are usually dirty and sometimes are the wrong size for cooking small pieces of meat. Once you have used a grill from home for this purpose, carry it in a paper sack or wrap it in newspaper, and put this parcel in a plastic garbage bag to keep it from blackening other gear. Or, you can take along an inexpensive portable one. If you burn wood instead of charcoal, the principle of laying and maintaining a fire are the same as for a campfire.

Charcoal, however, works the best. Use discretion, but soak the charcoal thoroughly with lighter fluid before lighting.

You do not need a recipe for barbecued meat. Treat yourself to some meat, cook and season as you would at home, and enjoy.

CAMP STOVE COOKING

Cooking on the camp stove is like cooking on top of your range at home. Frying an egg, boiling water for packaged soup or spaghetti, and heating up a jar of spaghetti sauce are just a few things that are quick and easy to do on a camp stove.

If you are at a high altitude, cooking takes more time because the air pressure is lower. Changes in the time required for cooking begin to occur at about 2,000 feet. At sea level water boils at 212 degrees Fahrenheit, but it drops one degree for each 500 feet above 2,000 feet. The result is that water must boil somewhat longer at higher altitudes than it does at sea level to properly cook food.

When you are using your camp stove in windy or cold weather, there will be considerable loss of heat, so it will take longer to prepare a meal. Some stoves have a built-in windscreen.

Pots of Gold

Serve as a main dish with a vegetable and/or salad.

1 package dried onion soup (size that yields 20 ounces of soup)
6 cups water
1/4 pound cheddar cheese
2 1/4 cups biscuit mix
Scant 2/3 cup milk

1. Place the dried soup in a saucepan with the water and bring to a boil, covered.

2. Dice cheese into 1-inch cubes, yielding 9 cubes.

3. Make biscuit dough by stirring the biscuit mix and milk together until it is well combined. Take 1 heaping tablespoon of dough and pinch it into a circle, about 1/8 inch thick. Place a cube of cheese in the middle and bring the dough up around it, sealing the edges. Roll it in your palms into a tight, round ball.

4. Place 3 dough packages at a time in the boiling broth, cover, and boil for 3 minutes. Take out carefully with a slotted spoon.

Yield: 9 pots of gold

Camper's Coffee

There is no reason to fear that camping vacations mean instant or no coffee. Make the real thing, and right on the campfire.

8–10 ounces water per serving
1 heaping tablespoon ground coffee per serving

Fill your coffee pot with the desired amount of water and coffee grounds. Bring to boil. Remove from heat and let grounds settle. Pour.

When it is convenient, use your campfire to make coffee. It is festive and saves fuel. If your campfire does not have a grill to set the pot on, put a rock in the campfire (or place a grill on two rocks) and set your coffee pot on it. When the coffee comes to a rolling boil, remove the pot, using an oven mitt. Set the pot aside on a warm, level spot for the grounds to settle and to keep the coffee warm.

Hard-Boiled Eggs

Make these in the morning for the afternoon picnic, or at night for breakfast.

Eggs
Water for boiling
Salt

Put eggs in cold water to which a little salt has been added. (If the shell breaks, the salt keeps the crack from getting any bigger.) Using a medium to low flame, bring the eggs to a boil. Boil on a low flame for 10 minutes. Take them out and douse them in cold water. Turn once or twice so the yolks will settle in the middle.

Tomato Rarebit

Served over toast, English muffins, or biscuits from your biscuit mix, Tomato Rarebit makes a good main dish. Serve it with a vegetable and/or salad.

1 can condensed tomato soup
1/3 cup milk
1/2 pound American cheese, sliced (about 12 slices) or diced
1 egg
1/2 –1 cup dried or precooked meat

1. Warm the soup and milk in a saucepan. Add the cheese and stir, over a low flame, until the cheese is melted.
2. Beat the egg in a small bowl with a wire whisk, then stir it slowly into the cooking mixture.
3. Add the meat, warming it through before serving.

Yield: 4 servings

Swiss Fondue

1 clove garlic
2 cups dry white wine
1 1/2 pounds Swiss cheese, grated or cut into small pieces
2 teaspoons cornstarch
1/4 cup Kirsch
Pinch of pepper
French bread cut into 1-inch cubes

1. Rub the inside of a cooking pot with the garlic, then discard the garlic.

2. Add the wine to the pot and heat over medium flame.

3. Add the cheese, stirring constantly until smooth. When bubbles begin to appear, mix together the cornstarch and Kirsch, then add to the pot, stirring constantly. Season with pepper. Keep the fondue slightly bubbling.

4. Spear bread cubes with a fork and dip into mixture to eat.

Yield: 6 servings

Pita Pizza

Make as many pizzas as you like with this simple camping recipe. Each round of pita makes two pizzas.

Whole wheat or white pita bread
Oil for frying
Tomato sauce for pizza
Cheese
Toppings

1. Cut each pita in half along the edge of the circle. You now have 2 pizza crusts.

2. Place pitas in an oiled fry pan, and spread on sauce and your favorite pizza cheese(s) and toppings. Cover with a lid to melt the cheese. You can regulate the texture of the crust by raising or lowering the temperature and/or removing the lid.

Biscuit Mix Pizza

Campsite pizza night!

2 1/4 cups biscuit mix
2/3 cup milk
Oil for frying
Tomato sauce for pizza
Cheese
Toppings (such as Parmesan cheese, dehydrated green peppers, and bacon bits)

1. In a mixing bowl, combine biscuit mix with milk and stir until it forms a ball. Divide into 4 equal portions. With floured hands, pat each portion into a 5- to 6-inch circle.

2. Place one portion in an oiled pan (about 1 tablespoon) over medium-low heat. Cook for about a minute, or until lightly browned. Be careful, as it burns easily. Lift with spatula, add another tablespoon of oil, and turn over. Spread with sauce, add the cheese and toppings, and cover. Cook for about 2 minutes, melting the cheese and browning the crust.

Yield: 4 6-inch pizzas

Fruit Cobbler

This is a winner for breakfast, dinner dessert, or that last, warm, high-in-carbohydrates snack before bedtime. Basically it is dumplings topped with sugar and cooked over canned fruit.

2 cups biscuit mix
2/3 cup milk

2 15 1/4-ounce cans of pineapple, chunks or crushed, or a 21-ounce can pie filling

1/4 to 1 cup brown, granulated, or powdered sugar

1. In a mixing bowl, stir together biscuit mix and milk. It should be a wet dough.

2. Pour undrained fruit into a 10-inch frying pan and heat just to boiling. Lower the flame. Spoon 8 equal mounds of batter on top of the fruit. Sprinkle on the sugar to taste. Cover and simmer for about 10 minutes.

3. Serve in bowls.

Yield: 8 servings

Hush Puppies

If you think deep-frying is messy at home, you will not mind it at camp. Remember, peanut oil can come to a higher temperature than other oils before smoking, making it the best to use for deep-frying. Serve these hush puppies with dinner and have strawberry jam available.

1 1/4 cups yellow cornmeal

1 teaspoon salt

1 teaspoon onion salt (optional)

3/4 teaspoon baking soda

3/4 cup buttermilk (or make sour milk by gently adding 1 teaspoon vinegar to 3/4 cup milk and letting it stand to thicken)

Oil for deep-frying

1. Mix the cornmeal, salts, and baking soda in a bowl. Add buttermilk and mix well.

2. Heat about 1/2 to 1 inch of oil in a skillet or Dutch oven. Drop the batter into the oil by heaping tablespoonfuls. Fry about 2 minutes,

until well browned. If the oil does not quite cover them as they cook, turn them over with two teaspoons after a minute.

3. Put hush puppies in a basket or bowl lined with paper towels and serve.

Yield: 15–20 hush puppies

PIT COOKING

The pit-cooking method involves slow cooking a meal in a cast-iron pot that has been buried in a pit of hot coals. Pit cooking is convenient because it is like using a crock pot. What fun to come back to the campsite after a day of recreation and smell the aroma of a cooking meal.

A cast-iron Dutch oven is perfect, but you can use any cast-iron pan with a cast-iron lid that has been seasoned according to manufacturer's directions.

Scrape the ashes from the campsite's fire pit to the edge, going into the dirt just an inch or less. Throw in a ten-pound bag of barbecue briquets and burn it to the white stage.

Now prepare the pot for the pit.

On a table, lay out overlapping newspapers about three sheets thick, making a surface of about 24 inches by 36 inches. Wet the papers, set the filled pot in the center, and bring the papers up to wrap the pot. Slip the wrapped pot into a paper bag to secure the bundle. Wrap the bundle in foil, using about four strips 36 inches long and wrapping each strip in a different direction.

Using your shovel, move all but a single layer of the white coals to the edges. Place the kettle on the coals in the center. With the shovel, pack the remaining coals around the kettle. Mound the ashes that you scraped away in the beginning around the coals; you can use a little dirt too. Make sure that no smoke escapes, allowing the fire to burn out prematurely.

The cooking time depends on what you are cooking and the intensity of the fire—from four to eight hours.

To recover the pot, carefully scrape away the ashes, the dirt, and the coals so that your shovel does not disturb the lid.

Use one of the following recipes to fill your cast-iron pot.

Bean-Hole Beans

About 2 cups dried beans, any type
1 teaspoon baking soda
1 to 2 onions
Salt
1 to 2 pounds ham, sandwich meat, or hot dogs, cubed or sliced
Seasoning preferences (catsup, tomato sauce, garlic, chili powder, 1/4 cup brown sugar, and/or 1/4 cup molasses

1. Wash and pick over the beans. Place them in the cast-iron Dutch oven and add water to at least 3 inches above the top of the beans. Soak overnight.

2. In the morning, drain; put beans back in pot and cover with fresh water to about 2 inches from the top for a 4-quart pot (about 5 cups), add baking soda. Simmer on the camp stove for about 15 minutes. Then add the onions, salt, meat, and other seasonings to taste. The contents should be 1 to 1 1/2 inches from the top of the pot.

3. Wrap the Dutch oven and, wearing gloves, place it in the prepared pit. Cover with coals, ashes, and dirt. Allow to bake for 6 hours or more.

Yield: 6–8 servings

Pot Roast or Stew

About 4 pounds meat (pot roast, stew, steak), cut up or left whole
Potatoes, carrots, onions, green pepper, tomatoes, and/or celery to taste, cut up or left whole

Seasonings to taste (salt, pepper, garlic, wine, dehydrated soup, and/or tomato sauce)

3 to 6 cups water

1. Braise meat in 1 to 2 tablespoons of oil, if desired. Fill Dutch oven with the meat, vegetables, seasonings, and water. The pot can be filled to 1 1/2 inches from the top. Put on lid.

2. Prepare pit, wrap Dutch oven, and, wearing gloves, place pot on coals. Cover pot with coals, ashes, and dirt. Allow to bake for 6 hours or more.

Yield: 6–8 servings

SOURDOUGH

Sourdough is perfect for campers, just as it was for the pioneers. Early settlers used it because they did not have refrigeration or dry yeast. Sourdough starter was their only way to transport yeast. Now, when camping, you can take advantage of the unique, tangy flavor of sourdough by toting it along. You can duplicate an authentic pioneering atmosphere with a classic sourdough pancake breakfast.

Sourdough, a living yeast, is nature's leavening agent. In the baking process, its culture of natural organisms multiply and grow in the starter and produce carbon dioxide bubbles, which become trapped in the dough and make it rise. This sourdough leavening is called a starter.

If you use your sourdough starter constantly, storage is not a problem. Like the pioneers, you keep it out between usage to get bubbly. However, if you do not use it every day, storage is necessary. Starter will last in the refrigerator up to one week. It will last in the freezer up to three months. To use refrigerated or frozen starter, it must be left out for twelve hours or overnight in a warm spot (85 degrees Fahrenheit is best) so that it gets bubbly. Store starter in a loosely covered jar, crock, or ridged plastic refrigerator dish that is twice the size of the starter.

Every time you use some starter you must have some left over that you can replenish. There are two methods of replenishing a starter, before you use it or after you use it. If there is enough starter for a recipe and 1/2 cup left over for replenishing, simply take out the starter the night before you are going to cook and put it in a 85-degree place overnight. (Be careful when using the campfire for a warm spot, as temperatures above 95-degrees are very likely to kill your sourdough starter.) At cooking time, take out the starter needed for the recipe. Add two parts plain yogurt to one part flour to the remaining starter in the jar. Set this out until it gets bubbly and then either use it or store it.

A second method of replenishing a starter is to make a sponge (some call this primary batter) with your starter the night before you are going to cook. Put all the starter in a large clean bowl and add to it as much starter (two parts plain yogurt to one part flour) as you are going to use in your recipe. Stir it all together, cover the bowl, and set it out overnight in a warm place. In the morning return to the storage jar what you do not use in your recipe and refrigerate.

Sourdough Starter

2 cups flour
4 cups plain yogurt
1 package active dry yeast dissolved in 1/4 cup warm
water (optional)

Mix all the ingredients in a bowl that is twice the size of the ingredients. Cover with plastic wrap. Let stand in a warm place (85 degrees) for about 48 hours, assuming the temperature can be maintained. The starter is ready when it doubles in size and gets bubbly; stir down once or twice in the middle of the process. Put it in a loosely covered jar or crock and refrigerate until ready to use. Replenish what you use with two parts yogurt to one part flour.

Yield: 5–6 cups

Sourdough Pancakes

Remember that the starter must sit in a warm place overnight before you use it.

1 1/4 cup flour
1 tablespoon baking powder
1/2 teaspoon baking soda
1 tablespoon sugar (optional)
1/2 teaspoon salt
1–2 cups starter
1 egg
1 1/4 cups milk
1/4 cup oil plus oil for the pan

1. Mix the flour, baking powder, baking soda, sugar, and salt together in a large bowl. Mix the starter, egg, milk, and 1/4 cup oil together in a separate bowl. Combine the two mixtures.

2. A griddle covering two burners is perfect. Grease the pan by rubbing it with oil, and bring to medium heat. Test for this temperature: A few drops of cold water will bounce and dance on the pan; if they immediately turn to steam, the temperature is too hot; if they lie there, the temperature is too cold.

3. Cook pancakes on medium heat in dollar-size portions until golden brown; turn and cook second side until golden.

Yield: 4 servings

Note: If you have batter left over, use it another morning. You can refrigerate it a couple of days, then add enough milk to make it the right consistency again, if necessary.

Sourdough Skillet Cornbread

You are baking on the open fire using a Dutch oven. Make this bread when the fire will have a nice, hot spot for about 1 1/2 hours. Use gloves and your shovel to prepare the right ovenlike spot, using some rocks if necessary for leveling and arranging the glowing wood and coals. When you experience the thrill of a whole kettle of beautiful, mounded, golden cornbread, you're likely to go camping again just to make it again. No fair cooking it at home! Serve it with beans, soup, stew, salad, or barbecued meat.

1 cup sourdough starter

3 cups yellow cornmeal

1 cup white or whole wheat flour

1/4 cup sugar

2 teaspoons salt

2 teaspoons baking soda

2 eggs

1/4 cup oil

1 1/2 cups milk

1. Set your starter out first thing in the morning if you plan to make this bread for dinner. Replenish the cup of starter that you will be using at this time or at baking time.

2. At dinnertime, thoroughly grease a seasoned cast-iron Dutch oven. Check that the fire is ready.

3. In a large mixing bowl, combine the five dry ingredients. In a small bowl combine the starter, eggs, oil, and milk. Mix all the ingredients together, and pour the mixture into the greased Dutch oven. Put on the lid.

4. Place the pot on the prepared fire spot. Try to simulate the conditions of a 350-degree oven. If necessary, make a tent of foil around the pot where the heat does not reach it. Wearing your gloves, shift

the position of the pot according to the blaze of the fire and to give all sides of the pot equal exposure to the fire. Test for doneness after 1 hour. If it looks done, test it with a clean stick in the middle. It will come up clean when the bread is thoroughly cooked. If it is not done, arrange a hotter fire, but be very careful not to burn the bread.

Yield: 8 big wedges

Sourdough Biscuits

1 cup sourdough starter
2 1/2 cups biscuit mix
1 cup flour
1/2 teaspoon baking soda
1 teaspoon salt
1 cup milk

1. Set the starter out first thing in the morning if you plan to make these biscuits for dinner. Replenish the cup of starter that you will be using at this time or at baking time.

2. At dinnertime, combine the 4 dry ingredients in a large bowl. Mix the starter and milk together and combine with the dry ingredients.

3. Put batter into a liberally greased cast-iron Dutch oven. Spread evenly over the bottom. Put on lid.

4. Simulate a 350-degree oven in the campfire, choosing a level spot with glowing coals and wood that will warm as much surface as possible. If necessary, make a tent of foil around the pot where the heat does not reach it. Turn the pot so that all sides have equal exposure to the fire. Be careful not to burn. Remember that the fire might not be consistent, so watch carefully.

5. Check for doneness after 45 minutes. It is ready when golden.

Yield: 8 large wedges

8

Safety and First Aid

This chapter of selected first-aid procedures for campers *is not a substitute for professional medical care*. In an emergency, always seek medical help quickly.

Bring along an established text on first aid—the most recent edition of *The Standard First Aid and Personal Safety* by the American Red Cross (consult your local chapter for updated information) or a first-aid book from a bookstore or camping-supply store.

Sign up for the first-aid course offered by your local chapter of the American Red Cross. They offer basic and advanced programs and special training for cardiopulmonary resuscitation (CPR)—techniques for reviving victims of heart failure. This is important. CPR is the only approved procedure when there is no breathing or pulse, and it cannot be administered without training because using it unnecessarily or incorrectly can cause serious harm.

Consider a medical checkup for everyone before going on your camping trip. Adult campers should be immunized with tetanus antitoxin every ten years; children, every five years. Keep a family medical record of these innoculations and other helpful information when traveling.

You must pack first-aid supplies. You can purchase ready-made kits, or you may want to put together your own, which can be customized to suit your unique needs—size of family, individuals' ages, length of stay, location(s), and individual propensity to certain problems. Remember to keep first-aid items away from the children.

You might want to include the following in your first-aid kit:

- Thermometer
- Butterfly bandages
- Bandage strips (large and small)
- Elastic wraps
- Triangular sling
- Sterile gauze pads
- Sterile gauze rolls
- Adhesive tape
- Cotton swabs
- Cotton balls
- Moleskin
- Microphore tape
- Antiseptic cleansing pads
- Absorbent cotton
- Antiseptic soap
- Tweezers
- Scissors
- Safety pins
- Needle
- Lip salve
- Antibiotic ointment
- Local antiseptic for sun and sunburn relief
- Hydrogen peroxide
- Rubbing alcohol
- Sunscreen
- Insect repellent
- Foot powder

- Aspirin or acetaminophen
- Salt tablets
- Cortisone cream
- Calamine lotion
- Diarrhea remedy
- Antacid
- Antihistamine
- Constipation relief
- Water-purification tablets
- Flashlight with extra batteries and bulbs
- Baking soda
- Cold pack
- Vaseline
- Mineral oil
- Ipecac syrup and activated charcoal
- Sharp knife or razor blade
- Eye patch
- Tongue blades and wooden applicator sticks
- Prescription medication (watch expiration date)
- Throat lozenges or throat spray
- Stretchy, foam-backed tape
- Anti-sting stick

Be familiar with the following alphabetical listing of first-aid precautions and practices. It is a handy reference guide tailored to a camper's needs—how to prevent camping-orientated hazards and first aid for accidents and ailments prevalent with campers.

In an emergency situation, send someone for medical aid. Emergency medical aid (paramedics or emergency medical technicians) may be dispatched from a fire department, a voluntary organization, a private company that has been contracted with a city or town, or sometimes from the local hospital. In many areas of the United States you can dial a 911 emergency number (even from a pay phone without inserting a coin) and receive immediate help. You should be prepared to give exact details, beginning with your location. Be certain you have given all the necessary information before you hang up; it is a good guide rule to let the other party hang up first. While you wait for help, tend to the victim with reassurance and gentleness. Maintain the victim's normal body temperature.

Most camping accidents happen for lack of basic safety. A safe trip is the result of caution, planning, and savvy—such as described in this listing.

FIRST-AID METHODS AND PRECAUTIONS FOR CAMPING-RELATED ACCIDENTS AND AILMENTS

Altitude Sickness

The body reacts to lack of oxygen at high altitudes, beginning at an approximate elevation of 10,000 feet. The symptoms are headache, shortness of breath, loss of appetite, and nausea. These symptoms are only nuisances. More acute mountain sickness, however, is highly dangerous.

Acute mountain sickness can develop into cerebral edema, which is an accumulation of fluids in the brain. The headache turns violent, and the person staggers. Mountain sickness can also develop into high-altitude pulmonary edema, which is an accumulation of fluid in the lungs. The symptoms are like pneumonia—coughing, shortness of breath, and tight-feeling lungs. In both cases, get the victim to a lower elevation. A drop of a couple of thousand feet will bring some recovery. Keep the hiker alert; bed rest makes the condition worse.

To avoid altitude sickness, ascend slowly, climbing no more than

1,000 feet per day. Take rest stops, take deep breaths during the rest stops, and eat simple sugar such as oranges and dried fruit.

People with heart and lung problems should consult their doctors before going to high altitudes.

Appendicitis

The symptoms are abdominal pain around the navel that later shifts to the lower right abdomen, nausea, sometimes vomiting, and a slight fever. All can develop over a few hours. The patient feels definite tenderness and pain when the abdomen is pressed. If these symptoms occur, get help right away. Do not assume that the pain is due to something the camper ate.

Bee Stings (see Insect Stings.)

Bites, Animal (See Puncture Wounds.)

Note here the additional danger of rabies. A skunk is the wild animal most likely to transmit rabies. Beware of any animal that acts oddly, including one that seems overfriendly. If you can get the animal (dead or alive) to the doctor with you, a lab analysis of it will determine if you need treatment.

Blisters

You will need to use some stretchy foam-backed tape that stays put or a specialized padded, adhesive product for blisters to form a home for the blister or hot spot, building up a protrusion around it for protection. You also can get a product that is a gelatin sheet packaged like a fruit roll. Cut it to size and peel off the backing, leaving a mucus to apply to the blister or hot spot. Cover this with an athletic tape that comes with it.

Catch blisters at an early stage—when you feel the soreness. If you do not, you will ruin the excursion for yourself and your companions.

Prevent blisters by wearing shoes that do not hurt, tying the laces just right, and wearing two pairs of socks—cotton next to the skin to absorb perspiration and wool for the outer sock to provide cushioning. Keep your socks dry and wrinkle free.

If you get a blister, wash the area with soap and water and dry it thoroughly before applying one of the above remedies.

Bruises

Bruising is due to bleeding into the tissues, which causes swelling and discoloration. It is usually caused by a physical injury, so make sure that there is no other damage. If the swelling is accompanied by severe pain or becomes more painful and/or swollen after the first twenty-four hours, take the victim to a hospital for further examination. Otherwise, rest the area in an elevated position and apply a cold compress to reduce the swelling.

Burns (See also Sunburn.)

First aid for burns is intended to prevent shock and infection and to alleviate pain. Immerse the burn in cold water for fifteen to twenty minutes. If the burn is severe, take the victim to a medical facility. Otherwise, cover the burn with wet gauze, if desired, and ice.

For superficial burns, apply burn ointments either directly on the burn or on a sterile gauze pad placed on the burn. Antiseptic sprays with an anesthetic for pain relief are a must.

Cuts

Wash cuts with soap and water. Apply an antibiotic ointment or spray. Apply a nonstick dressing.

If you need to stop the bleeding, apply (using a clean dry cloth) direct, continuous pressure over the wound for at least five minutes. Elevate if possible. Hold minor cuts together with a butterfly tape from the first-aid kit. These are used on a clean, dry, and antiseptic-coated wound.

Diarrhea (See also Giardiasis.)

Diarrhea can be caused by a change in diet, such as an excess of fruit, spices, or rich food, or a viral infection. It also can be caused by Giardia (a parasite that enters the intestines, which is carried in clean-looking water). First aid for diarrhea is limited to replacing the lost fluid and taking a pectin medicine.

Earache

Do not put anything in the ear such as a cotton swab, paper clip, fingernail, or ointment or drops. Any of these might do harm or interfere with the doctor's examination of the ear canal.

Earaches of short duration can have a number of causes, such as water in the ear or a sudden change of altitude. Any earache that persists for an hour or two, without decreasing in intensity, warrants medical attention. Give aspirin or acetaminophen.

Most ear pain is caused by infection, and you must take the victim to a doctor right away so that he can prescribe an antibiotic.

If the earache is caused by an insect, you may be able to bring out the offending bug by shining a flashlight into the ear. Apply heat and have the victim chew gum to keep the ear passages open. Do not try to remove an object or insect from an ear. You might force it farther down and cause added injury. Take the victim to medical help for this.

Eyes

In the case of chemical burns, irrigate the eye with water right away, while someone else makes preparations for medical help. To irrigate, wash the eyes with a gentle stream of cold running water poured from a cup or glass or the hand from two to three inches above the eye. Keep irrigating until you are sure the chemical has been completely removed. Adults may use a shower. Never put medications of any kind into an injured eye without a physician's order. Cover the injured eye or eyes with a dry, sterile gauze pad.

Foreign bodies are the most common cause of eye injuries. Do not rub the eye or pick at it. Try to wash out the foreign body with water. If you can see it, try lightly to dislodge it with a moistened, sterilized cotton swab. Have the victim wear sunglasses for a day so that the sunlight does not irritate the eye.

Fainting

Fainting is a partial or complete loss of consciousness due to temporary reduction in the blood supply to the brain. Recovery of consciousness almost always occurs when the person falls or is placed in a reclining position (although injury may occur from the fall).

Look for the following symptoms for preventive care. Treat these symptoms as if the faint occurred:

- Extreme paleness
- Sweating
- Cold skin
- Dizziness
- Nausea
- Vision disturbances
- Numbness and tingling in hands and feet

When a person has fainted, do the following:

- Lay victim down with the lower legs somewhat elevated, leaving him where he has fainted

- Loosen any tight clothing and keep crowds away

- If the victim vomits, roll him onto his side or turn his head to the side, and if necessary, wipe out his mouth with your fingers wrapped in cloth

- Maintain an open airway, especially if convulsions occur

- Do not pour water over the victim's face (he may breathe in water); bathe face gently with cool water

- Do not give liquids unless the victim has revived

- Examine the victim for injuries

- Seek medical assistance if recovery is not prompt

Fishhook

You may fish your entire life and never face the unpleasant task of removing a fishhook.

Before beginning, deaden the pain by applying ice or very cold water to the general area of the wound. Have the victim look the other way.

Push the barb (the triangular flange at the point) all the way through the finger—like sewing with a needle—and clip it off. Pull the shaft of the hook back out with a pair of pliers.

This type of wound is susceptible to the tetanus bacterium. See a doctor as soon as possible.

Food Poisoning (See Poisoning.)

Giardiasis

Giardia is a parasite that enters the intestine. It is transmitted by contaminated water and direct person-to-person contact. It is found in wild animals, and there have been outbreaks across the United States.

The infection (sometimes called "beaver fever") causes diarrhea, gas, loss of appetite, cramps, bloating, and sometimes fever. It can last ten days or more, and it can reappear after many months. You must go to a doctor for a prescription to fight the intestinal bacteria, and treat as for diarrhea.

The infection can be present with no symptoms, in which case the person is a carrier of the infection and can unknowingly infect others. The symptoms appear seven to ten days after infection. Take the preventive approach and treat the drinking and cooking water that you use from streams. Wash your hands before cooking and eating and after using the toilet.

Headache

A headache indicates a change in the body. It is a warning that something is wrong. When you are camping, headaches can be caused by:

- Altitude or mountain sickness
- Water glare and bright sunlight
- Tension
- Insect bites
- Heat exhaustion
- Dehydration
- Lack of sleep
- Overexcitement
- Hunger
- Change in the weather

Additional causes are:
- Allergy
- Toothache
- Alcohol
- Depression
- Sinus trouble

Treat the headache with aspirin or acetaminophen.

Try massage, hot or cold packs, hot baths, rest, quiet, shade, and removal of stress. If the pain lingers, changes drastically, or is accompanied by fever, paralysis, weakness, numbness, double vision, or speech impairment, go to a doctor.

Heat Exhaustion

Heat exhaustion is a result of prolonged exposure to high temperatures, which cause the body to lose important fluids and salt. This produces a fall in blood pressure and decreases the blood supply to the brain. The symptoms are white, clammy skin; weakness; dizziness; headache, but normal temperature.

Treat carefully to prevent heat stroke, which is very dangerous. If the victim is conscious, place him in a cool environment and have him lie down with his feet raised about eight to twelve inches; remove and/or loosen clothing and fan; give him sips of cool salt water (one teaspoon of salt to one glass of water), and sponge him with water.

If the victim vomits, do not give any more fluids. Get him to medical aid where an intravenous salt solution can be given. Advise the victim to rest for several days and to stay protected from abnormally warm temperature.

Heat Stroke

Anyone who has been exposed to heat or the direct rays of the hot sun for one to several hours, and who develops a temperature of 100 to 105 degrees or higher, should be suspected of having heat stroke (unless the fever can be otherwise explained). The symptoms are:

- Hot, blushed, dry skin
- Weakness
- Headache
- Dizziness
- Muscular twitching
- Nausea
- Vomiting
- Strong, rapid pulse
- Absence of sweating

Heat stroke can be fatal unless recognized early and treated. The purpose of first aid is to cool down the body quickly without chilling. First, reduce the victim's temperature to 100 to 102 degrees by undressing him and sponging his skin with cool water. Give aspirin or acetaminophen. Dry him off when the temperature has been reduced. Fan the victim and continue checking his temperature every fifteen minutes for one hour; his temperature should continue to go down until it is normal. If the victim is conscious, give him cool salt water to sip (one teaspoon of salt to one glass of water). Call a doctor. Do not be fooled by temporary relief. Further examination is necessary.

Think about prevention for heat stroke. Be sure you and your camping group get enough salt, water, rest, and cooling. If you sweat a lot, be sure to take extra water and extra salt. Rest more often and sit in the shade to cool down. The sun can overheat the scalp very quickly and do damage. Keep your head covered when you have to be out in the sun for any length of time. Hair shades the scalp a bit, but not as well as a large, well-ventilated hat.

Hypothermia

Hypothermia is the loss of body heat. When the body's temperature drops more than 3 degrees below normal 98.6 to 98.4 degrees Fahrenheit, changes occur, which can lead to death. A preliminary shivering, with cold feet and hands, begins when the body's temperature is at 96 degrees and above. Later the shivering becomes uncontrollable. Shivering consumes energy reserves until they are exhausted. When this happens, cold reaches the brain, and the victim loses judgment and reasoning power.

When the body becomes chilled, it begins to reduce circulation to the skin and to the extremities in order to maintain the proper temperature in the vital organs at the core of the body. The inner core must be kept at a steady temperature (98.4 to 98.6 degrees Fahrenheit).

The conditions that cause heat loss are: lack of physical conditioning (exhaustion); a cold environment; wind; and wetness caused by rain, snow, or sweat. A temperature of 50 degrees Fahrenheit can be treacherous in these conditions. Time has no mercy. Hypothermia can begin in a matter of minutes and, if untreated, cause death in two hours.

Although the subject of hypothermia is usually dealt with for backpackers in remote high country, when walking for long periods of time under poor conditions—low temperature, wind, wetness, exhaustion—the beginning camper is vulnerable, too. Campers encounter unexpected cold nights, immersion in cold water, wind at 50 degrees Fahrenheit, and variable weather conditions when hiking. Be cautious. If you dress properly for warmth, stay dry (your head is especially important) so that the body temperature does not drop, and be aware of the wind, you will not get this No. 1 killer.

The symptoms are: normal to uncontrolled, violent shivering (some victims, such as those who are overtired, do not shiver), difficulty in speaking or slurred speech, mental deterioration and irrational thinking, loss of muscular control (stumbling), unconsciousness, drowsiness (to sleep is to die), and apparent exhaustion, such as an inability to get up after a rest.

When treating for hypothermia, be firm about the procedure. The victim cannot identify his problem and will often say or insist he is okay. All treatment is designed to rebuild the lost body heat. Warm the victim's clothing, warming him by a fire and/or in a sleeping bag that is warmed with someone in it, or find a sheltered spot. Give the victim something warm to drink. Keep him awake. Constantly monitor for breathing difficulty and consciousness. Handle frostbitten parts gently and protect them from further injury. Handle the victim gently, because jolts may initiate a heart attack. Immediately get to hospital care. Hypothermia drains both body and spirit, so give plenty of rest after the danger has passed.

Infections

Signs that a wound is infected are:

- Swelling and redness
- Sensation of heat
- Throbbing pain
- Tenderness
- Fever
- Pus
- Red streaks leading from the wound

If any wound is infected, get prompt medical care. If there is a delay, treat the infection by having the victim lie down and elevate the infected area. Keep the victim and especially the wound area still. Apply warm packs directly to the infected area, using warm, moist towels. Take the victim's temperature several times and be prepared to give that information to the doctor.

Insect Stings and Bites

If you know you are sensitive (allergic) to the venom of a specific insect, carry a special emergency kit with instructions. Severe reactions to an insect bit (anaphylaxis) will likely show up in a highly irritated rash, breathlessness, collapse, and shock. Get medical help immediately.

Bee stings are serious only if you are allergic to them. Signs of allergy are:

• Swelling that extends beyond two joints (except for fingers and toes)
• Headache
• Stomach pain, vomiting, diarrhea
• Fever
• Drowsiness, fainting, unconsciousness
• Spasms or convulsions

Sometimes there is a delayed reaction—as long as two weeks following the sting.

If the victim is allergic and does not have medication, get medical help, and take the following steps:

• If the sting is on a leg, do not allow the victim to walk on it
• Keep the affected part below the level of the heart
• Apply cold cloths to the site of the sting
• If the victim's breathing is weak, or if his lips or fingernails are bluish in color, apply mouth-to-mouth resuscitation.

• Remove the stinger by gently scraping it out with a sharp object such as a knife or your fingernail. Do not use tweezers or fingers to grasp the stinger because this may squeeze more venom into the sting.

Treat minor stings and mild reactions by removing the stinger and washing the area with soap and water. Daub it with antiseptic or anti-sting stick and apply cold compresses (cloths) for about thirty minutes and then a paste of baking soda and water.

When itching starts, apply rubbing alcohol, after-shave lotion, or calamine lotion.

Prevent bites by wearing a repellent containing N. N-Diethyl-meta-toluamide (deet). With it on the skin, insects will land but not bite. If insects are a problem around your face, try spraying a bandanna with insect repellent and tying it around your neck.

Nosebleed

Sit up and pinch the nostrils or press on the side that is bleeding. Hold for five minutes.

If bleeding does not stop, put a small cone of cotton or soft tissue into the nostril that is bleeding. If the bleeding continues, try cold packs over the bridge of the nose.

When bleeding stops, leave the cold packs in place for a while and/or rest quietly. Do not blow or rub the nose, sniff hard, or pick at the encrusted blood for some time after.

Poisoning

Begin first aid immediately. Seek medical assistance. If possible, have someone call the local poison control center. In some states, you can call 911 and be immediately connected. Or, dial 0, and when you say it is an emergency, they will transfer you. Give the following information:

• Age of the victim

• Name of the poison and the amount taken, if known, or the general nature of the drug or chemical

- First aid being given
- Your location, the time it will take to get to the physician or the hospital, and whether a police escort will be necessary

If the victim is unconscious, maintain an open airway and give artificial respiration. Do not give fluids, and do not induce vomiting. If the victim is vomiting, position him and turn his head so that the material drains out of the mouth.

The symptoms for poisoning are:

- Abdominal discomfort
- Diarrhea
- Severe nausea
- Vomiting
- Chills, fever
- Weakness

If the victim is conscious, dilute the poison by giving him a glass of water or milk (up to a quart for ages five to adult, and half of a quart for children under five). Discontinue if the liquid makes him nauseated.

The local poison control center will instruct you based on what was swallowed. Syrup of ipecac is used to induce vomiting. If it is not available, you will have to tickle the back of the victim's throat with a finger or blunt end of a spoon after giving water. Activated charcoal is for binding (deactivating) the poisonous substances.

With food poisoning, prevention is the key. Keep all cooking and serving utensils clean. Make sure your hands are thoroughly washed before you handle and prepare food. Keep your ice chest cold; bacteria thrive at temperatures between 40 and 140 degrees Fahrenheit.

Never eat wild plants and shellfish unless you are absolutely certain of their identity. Poisonous mushrooms may grow where nonpoisonous mushrooms grow. Shellfish such as mussels, clams, oysters, and abalone are potentially poisonous if eaten during the months of June through October.

In cases of food poisoning, call for medical help immediately and induce vomiting if vomiting has not already begun. Do not give the victim anything to eat or drink until his vomiting and diarrhea have stopped.

Poison Oak, Ivy, and Sumac

These are primarily regional plants, so you might need to learn to identify only one of them. The approximate regions for each are from the Pacific Ocean to the Cascade and Sierra mountains—poison oak; east of the Cascades, east of the Rockies, and lake shores—poison ivy; and swamps—poison sumac.

Poison oak and poison ivy are similar in appearance. The leaves of both are in clusters of three, have the appearance of an oak leaf, and turn red in the autumn. The differences are that poison oak is a shrub or tree and poison ivy is a vine, and that poison oak's leaves are lobed between the points, while the leaves of poison ivy have a jagged edge. Poison sumac is a tall shrub with smooth leaves that grow in a single line along the stem and opposite one another. The leaves turn red in the autumn. All three plants have white berries in the summer.

These plants secrete a poisonous oil that is present in all parts of the plant, including dead stems and roots. It may be picked up by direct contact or transmitted from handling contaminated clothing, tools, animals, and the like, or from exposure to the smoke when the plant is burned.

Symptoms usually appear within one or two days after contact. The skin will burn and itch, feel bumpy, and eventually form blisters, and in severe cases, swelling. If the oils have been inhaled, the symptoms will include swelling of the tissues in the nose, throat, and lungs. Respiratory difficulties may develop, and they require immediate professional care.

To treat, remove all contaminated clothing, including shoes, belt, and backpack. Wash the affected skin with soap and water. (Use a strong laundry soap or detergent. Ordinary bathroom soap will only spread the oil and the itching.) Avoid scratching, which can lead to a secondary infection. Apply ice-water compresses and/or a soothing lotion such as calamine or a cortisone cream to the affected areas. Apply these medications thinly and avoid covering too much of the body's surface; be careful around the eyes. If these lotions are not available, use rubbing alcohol or a thick paste of soap. If blistering and oozing develop, apply two tablespoons of salt in a pint of water with cold, wet compresses.

Puncture Wounds

Puncture wounds are caused when objects such as nails, fishhooks, knives, and ice picks penetrate the skin. The point of entry may be small, but arteries and nerves may be damaged. Wounds of this type may look harmless on the surface, producing very little external bleeding, but can cause serious deep injury and serious infections.

To treat, remove the cause of the wound. Squeeze gently around the hole to make it bleed and to clean out any dirt. Wash the wound with soap and water, and apply an antibiotic and bandage.

Tetanus germs may have been carried into the wound. Tetanus is a serious complication of any injury. The tetanus bacterium may be introduced into the body when an injury becomes contaminated with soil, street dust, or animal or human waste. See a doctor; he may order a tetanus shot.

Snakebite

Preventing snakebites is your best defense. Knowledge of the snake's habits makes it easier to be on the alert. Learn to identify the poisonous snakes by using a field guide.

Fortunately, the great majority of snakes in the United States are nonpoisonous. The poisonous snakes are either pit vipers or coral snakes. Pit vipers include the water moccasin or cottonmouth snake, the copperhead or highland moccasin snake, and the thirteen species of rattlesnake—known by its rattles. There are two species of coral snakes in the United States, one in the Southeast and the other in southern Arizona. They are brilliantly colored.

Some poisonous snakes like to warm their cold blood on sunny slopes with rocky ledges and sandy stretches. However, when temperatures are high, they are more apt to be hidden in the shade. They are more active when temperatures are moderate. They avoid damp places except in the middle of the day when they seek streams to drink from or lie in wait for frogs, toads, and small rodents. The eastern coral snake travels during twilight, however; the pit viper is king of the swamps; and the water moccasin dwells in ponds. Usually snakes stay below 6,000 feet.

As a rule, snakes will try to avoid you. Unless surprised, hurt, or concerned, snakes will not attack. If you see a snake, keep your distance from it.

The rattlesnake can strike from a distance of one-half to two-thirds its length, but do not estimate a safe distance by this. Rattlesnakes can climb trees and bushes, and they can swim.

When camping, be alert for snakes. Know the outdoor terrain; watch where you sit, step, and stretch; and avoid reaching into holes or hidden ledges. Wear protective clothing such as boots, trousers, slacks, and sleeved shirts. Do not alarm a sleeping snake (even a newborn snake) or tease or molest an awake snake. Keep an eye on your **children**. They are inexperienced around snakes and may be careless while playing. Backpackers who go into the wilderness should carry a snakebite kit and read the enclosed instructions at the time of purchase instead of at the time of an accident.

Toxicity may vary among snakes of the same species, depending on the season and the snake's habitat. It is interesting that fifteen percent of all rattlesnake bites are not poisonous and another fifteen percent are of minor consequence.

Authorities agree on a few basic first-aid measures for poisonous bites:

- Get to a hospital as soon as possible
- Calm the victim
- Immobilize the injured limb at heart level, in a horizontal position

Spider Bite

Spiders in the United States are generally harmless. However, the black widow and the brown recluse, or violin spider, have bites that are dangerous. The black widow is about 3/4 inch to 1 1/2 inches long and is easily identified by the hourglass-shaped red spot on its belly. The brown recluse is from 1/2 to 3/8 inch long and looks something like an hourglass or violin on its underside. The tarantula is a large, hairy spider with a painful bite. Stings from scorpions are not usually considered serious. The scorpion is from 3/4 to 8 inches long and is solid yellow or yellow with black stripes on the back.

If spider bites cause a major reaction, treat the victim in the following manner:

- Immobilize the area and make the victim lie down
- Keep the affected part below the level of the heart
- Apply cold cloths or ice wrapped in a towel or plastic bag to decrease absorption of the poison and to relieve pain
- Transport the victim to a medical facility immediately
- If possible, be prepared with a description of the spider

Sprains

A sprain is damage to the soft tissue surrounding a joint. It is usually caused by a sudden twisting or wrenching of the joint, a direct blow, or a fall.

The symptoms of a sprain are swelling, tenderness, pain upon motion, and discoloration caused by blood escaping from the damaged vessels into the joint and surrounding tissues.

It is usually impossible to tell the difference between a sprain and a closed fracture without an X-ray. Small chip fractures often accompany the tissue injuries of a sprain.

Elevate the injury and keep it at absolute rest. Do this over a period of several days if needed. Apply cold, wet packs or place a small bag of crushed ice on the affected area over a thin towel to protect the skin, every twenty minutes every three or four hours. If swelling and pain persist, seek medical attention.

Strains

A strain is an injury to the muscle from overexertion. The muscle fibers are stretched and sometimes partially torn. Rest the area and apply heat.

Sunburn

Begin with prevention. Use preparations that protect against ultraviolet rays. A lotion with a sun protection factor of 15 permits you to remain in the sun fifteen times longer than normal before burning (as opposed to no lotion at all). Factors of 29 and 44 are very high on the scale. A factor of 15 is commonly used. Choose a lotion according to the sensitivity of your skin, how much tan you want, your concern about ultraviolet exposure, and the weather conditions. Remember that the burning power of sunlight is greater through the thin, clear air at high elevations.

A mild sunburn (first-degree burn) produces sore, red skin, without blisters. Keep the affected areas covered, wear a hat, and use sunburn lotions or oils.

A severe sunburn (second-degree burn) is marked by pain and blistering. Treat like other burns and do not exposure the skin to sunlight until it is completely recovered.

Block the eyes from the glare of the sun, sand, and water. Polarized sunglasses block out or cut the glare on a horizontal plane. This is why they are popular with drivers and people around masses of water—fishermen, boat passengers, and sunbathers. To check if a pair of glasses is polarized, rotate the glasses at 90 degrees. If the glare changes, they are polarized.

Another method of glare reduction is darkened glasses. They work best for general active use—hiking and sightseeing. These glasses should have UV protection, because ordinary darkened glasses open the pupils, allowing more ultraviolet rays to enter.

If it is difficult to keep glasses on your child, try attaching a rubber band to the ear pieces to form a grip.

Temperature

An elevated temperature is often due to cold-related ailments, which are not serious. Treat it with aspirin. However, a high temperature can also be a symptom of something more serious. Look for unusual symptoms and be aware of serious possibilities such as appendicitis and heat stroke. (See specific listings.)

Sponge the victim with cool water to reduce the fever and consult a doctor if you think it is a serious ailment.

Ticks

Begin with prevention. Be wary of ticks in the spring and summer. They are most plentiful in wooded lands and tall grass. They cling to the underside of leaves, brush, branches, and logs. They will drop on you as you walk through the forest or attach to you if you sit on an infested log. This small (1/8 to 1/4-inch), reddish brown bug with markings burrows into flesh and engorges on blood. It is wise to keep your skin as covered as possible when you are walking in tick territory. Wear clothes that fit snug at the neck and wrist and long socks over your pants. Tuck in your outer garment because the tick travels up. Wear light-colored clothing so you can see ticks easily. Every two hours during rest stops, search your body, having someone check your head, neck, and back. There is time for this; a tick normally explores for two hours before choosing a drill site. If you remove any clothing, do so over a light surface. If you see a tick drop, continue to look very carefully.

The tick buries its head in your skin and clings tenaciously. Do not pull it out carelessly; if the head remains, it will cause a nasty infection.

To remove it, apply oil (mineral, salad, or machine) to the body of the tick, which will interfere with its breathing. The tick may come off right away. If not, the oil will enable you to remove the tick completely without leaving its head embedded in the skin. Remove the tick with tweezers or your fingernails. (If fingers are used, they should be protected with tissue and washed afterward.) Do not jerk it out. Take your time so all parts of the tick come away. Do not dig ticks out. Save the tick to show a doctor if symptoms develop.

Scrub the area gently with soap and water because disease germs may be present on the skin.

See a doctor if the head of the tick remains in your skin and you develop infection, or if within two days to two weeks you get a headache, body aches, fever, and spots after one to three days of fever. The malady might be Rocky Mountain spotted fever, which you may find in the central and some eastern parts of the United States.

If the tick was very tiny and you get a rash, a headache, stiff neck, fever, muscle aches, swollen glands, and/or fatigue, it was probably a deer tick carrying Lyme disease. These symptoms may occur over a period of weeks. If you do not get treated for it . . . the rash will fade but complications will arise later. Lyme disease is mainly concentrated in the East, but it has spread into many other states.

Toenail Infection

There is one way to cut your toenails—straight across. Campers do a lot of walking. If the nails are cut at an angle, the tissue on either side of the nail tends to push over the nail. When the nail grows, it pushes into this skin, causing the nail to cut into the skin, resulting in infection. Treat a toenail infection with hot-water soaks. Consult a doctor.

Toothache

A warm saltwater mouthwash can help reduce pain and swelling. See a dentist as soon as possible. Take aspirin or acetaminophren.

9

Recreation

Because a campsite is not like Disneyland with its plentiful attractions, campers must be creative when planning their own amusement. For most families, after all, camping itself is insufficient as the sole activity for a vacation. Rather, camping takes you to a vacation spot, where you then take part in numerous activities that you consider fun. This chapter provides you with a selection of the many pursuits offered by nature.

HOBBIES THAT COMPLEMENT CAMPING

Nature-oriented hobbies provide a marvelous foundation for beginning campers, while advanced campers often put these hobbies to good use. Both beginning and advanced campers enjoy teaching and including their children in these nature-related hobbies.

Preferring to learn in a natural setting, children love learning these things. However, because this is a vacation, meet them on their own terms. If a hobby takes on the feeling of a school field trip, the children might rebel. Keep it light, and if it gets too tedious, move on to something else.

Most ranger stations have exhibits that call attention to the area's natural attractions. Sometimes they sponsor slide shows, lectures, campfire programs, and excursions. All of these activities enhance any nature-related hobby. Get resource material on the subjects that interest you. Camping stores, bookstores, and libraries have a supply on every topic.

Weather Observation

Weather is the governing factor for all outdoor activities. Usually weather forecasts are posted at the campground's ranger station. Advanced campers and backpackers need to know how to predict weather by looking at the sky and cloud formations; beginning campers would enjoy acquiring this knowledge. *All* campers must know about lightning in order to take the proper precautions when out in a storm.

SKY AND CLOUDS - Watching the sky and its cloud formations can be an ongoing hobby. Learn to identify types of clouds; there are three basic types. Cumulus clouds are lumpy, puffy, well rounded, and can look like a cauliflower. Stratus clouds are shaped in layers or sheets across the sky. Cirrus clouds are wispy. Clouds can be grouped into combinations of these basic types. Clouds also are identified by their height above the ground and their color tones.

LIGHTNING - Campers should be knowledgeable about lightning. The worst lightning storms take place in the mountains. Be familiar with the following information about lightning and the precautions you should take.

Lone, tall trees are dangerous; lightning flashes strike the tallest thing around. Single trees, ridges, and summits are all dangerous. Low trees or bushes are safe. Lightning strikes metal objects. Wire fences, umbrellas, and metal objects on you are all dangerous. Lightning is not attracted to water, but anything on a body of water will be an attraction. Do not be on or in the water.

If you get caught in a storm, and lightning is present, remove your backpack and anything else made of metal. Seek shelter under a *clump* of trees or in a building (away from the fireplace because lightning can travel down the chimney), car, or RV. Or get out in an open field and take a soaking. Crouch your feet close together to minimize the danger of ground current.

If you see lightning at a distance and hear the thunder, you can tell how far away the lightning is by counting the time between the flash and the thunder. Take about one second to say each count. Each count stands for about one fifth of a mile (or you can figure about 1,000 feet if that is easier). If you count to twenty-five, the lightning flash is about five miles away.

You can determine how fast the storm is approaching by waiting one minute and then counting another flash-to-thunder time. If the count has changed from twenty-five to twenty in the minute, the storm has moved one mile in the minute you waited. The storm is moving about sixty miles per hour, and you have about four minutes to find shelter.

Direction Finding—the Compass, the Sun, and the Stars

Even if you confine your explorations to well-populated state and national parks and stay on main trails, you can still get turned around. If you are an advanced camper or backpacker, you must be able to spot your position on a map and know where you are at all times. This is why direction finding is a perfect camping hobby.

THE COMPASS - Most family camping situations do not require a compass. Families usually stay near the major trails and camp-grounds. However, this is an opportunity to teach everyone in the family about the compass so that everyone is prepared to be an advanced camper. Get an orienteering compass.

It is fun if you are a beginning camper. Sometimes you lose your sense of direction in new territory. You can find the direction of home with your compass. When you are at the campsite and planning side trips, you can find the direction of your destinations. You can learn compass skills that are necessary for advanced camping—wilderness, backpacking, and snow.

Use the compass for holding your map in the right direction (orientating the map). Place the map on a flat surface. Now align the compass' straight edge (the longer side) with the north–south direction of the map. Rotate the map and the compass together until the compass needle is aligned with magnetic north. Now your map points in the right direction.

Also learn how to use this compass for determining the direction to walk toward so that you can get to a destination on the map.

1. Locate on the map where you are and your destination for practice, choose any destination. If this distance is more than three and a half inches long, use a straight edge along with your compass for the following. Place the compass's long edge (either side) on the dot where you are and on the dot that is your destination, with the direction-of-travel arrow on the compass pointing toward your destination.

2. Leaving the base plate there, rotate the compass housing so that the magnetic needle (floating red needle) is on top of the stationary arrow on the compass dial.

3. Take the compass off of the map and hold it level in front of you with the direction-of-travel arrow pointing away from you. Now turn yourself around until the magnetic needle is on top of the stationary arrow. Now the direction-of-travel arrow points to the destination. (See deviation material that follows.)

You just took a bearing reading on your compass. The bearing is a line of direction from one point to another measured in compass degrees. These degrees are marked on the compass dial where a line meets the base plate. You can read the position in degrees or in cardinal and intercardinal points such as N, S, W, E, and SW.

When you turned the housing to align north on the compass to north on the map, you were using a meridian line on the map. This line is any straight north to south line on the map.

You also used the compass for its most common use—working out bearings from the map to the compass. It is popular because it is so convenient to follow the bearing (direction of travel) while keeping the compass at north (floating needle on stationary needle).

Although an orienteering compass simplifies finding the bearing (direction of travel), you have to take into account the current, local (where you are) declination or variation. You do this by adding or subtracting degrees from the compass bearing.

The declination is the difference in degrees between the bearing of the compass needle (magnetic north) and the bearing of true north (geographic north). It is named declination or variation because the needle declines or varies east or west of true north, except on the agonic line.

The earth is a huge magnet with lines of force distributed between magnetic poles. It is this magnetism that furnishes the force that directs the compass needle. Magnetic poles, however, are not situated at the geographic poles.

The north magnetic pole is about 1,400 miles south and east of the geographic North Pole. The angle of difference between the geographic North Pole and magnetic north on the compass is declination.

The North Pole and magnetic north coincide at a line of zero degrees declination, technically called the agonic line. In the United States, this is a line approximately from Florida's east coast through Cincinnati, Ohio, Lake Michigan, and on up to near the Boothia Peninsula in Canada (Bathhurst Island north of Hudson Bay). From this line to the Atlantic Ocean (east), the compass naturally points west of true north, so you can compensate to the east. From this line to the Pacific Ocean (west), the compass naturally points east of true geographic north, so you can compensate to the west.

Your orienteering compass may have a feature to make the declination adjustment. Some models have a screw on the NE point of the housing and a tool for it attached to the red cord. Turn the screw to adjust the dial for the current declination of your location (current because declination changes with time, though not uniformly or consistently). Use the screw to move the stationary arrow (orienteering arrow) either east or west to the appropriate degrees for your location. There are special red markings inside the dial for this. Once adjusted, the housing, when turned to align north, will line up with declination taken into account.

A compass will not give a true reading when it is near a magnetic metal—iron or steel. Nonmagnetic metals—brass, copper, alu-

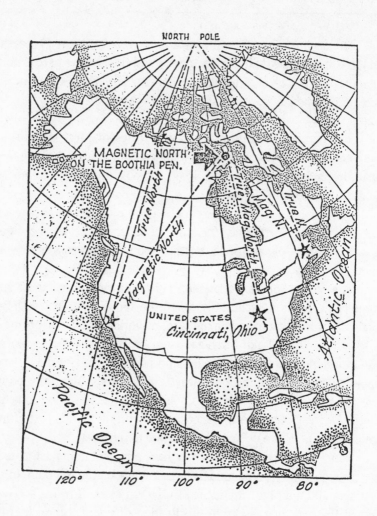

minum—will not affect the compass. Keep the compass away from another compass, a steel structure, a pocket knife, an ax, a flashlight, an exposure meter with photoelectric cells, power lines, and any motor vehicle.

If someone in the family is especially interested in the compass, help them pursue this ongoing hobby. They can learn direction-finding games and more advanced skills. For an orienteering teaching aids catalog and price list, write or call Orienteering Services, USA, Box 1504BL, Binghamton, NY 13902; (607)-724-0411.

THE SUN - Use the sun to find north. Children will enjoy learning this skill.

Put a watch that is set on standard time on a flat surface. If you do not have a watch, but know what time it is, draw a clock face on a piece of paper. Make it accurate. Trace a circle. Make four folds for the twelve, the three, the six, and the nine on the dial. Measure a segment's arc straight across from point to point and divide this into three. You can do this with a piece of paper. Use that amount for dividing the four arcs to fill in the clock face. Proceed as if it were a watch. Place a straight stick vertically at the center of the watch. Turn the watch until the shadow of the stick falls along the hour hand. This points the hour and the shadow directly away from the sun. North will then be midway between the hour hand and twelve o'clock.

At twelve noon (standard time) the sun is south, and its shadow points north. At noon set a stick in the ground where the sun can shine on it. The shadow points north. If you are at the campsite, lay another stick on the shadow as a marker for north.

On a sunny day, drive a stick into a section of flat ground. Slant it directly at the sun so that it makes no shadow. Within fifteen or twenty minutes a shadow will appear at the base of the stick. The shadow will point to the east. You can determine north from this. Do not take the stick out. Come back from time to time during the day to check the shadow. It will get longer and longer but will always be pointing east in the summer.

This shadow stick is most accurate in the summer when the sun is high overhead and least accurate in the winter when the sun is low in the southern sky.

THE STARS - Your family will enjoy an evening searching for the North Star—sometimes called Polaris or polestar. The axis of the earth points almost directly at the North Star; this star does not seem to move as the earth turns. All of the other stars appear to rotate around the North Star.

Begin by locating north with your compass or with one of the sun methods explained in the previous section. (When using your compass, remember to take in declination.) By locating north, you will know where in the sky to look for specific stars.

The Big Dipper circles the North Star about once every twenty-four hours. As the night progresses, the constellation is always in a different position. When it has moved a quarter of a circle around the North Star, you know that six hours have gone by. From late summer to early winter, portions of the Big Bear (the constellation to which the Big Dipper belongs) are below the northern horizon, or so near it that they cannot be seen. The bowl, however, is almost always visible.

Use the Big Dipper to guide you to the tip of the handle of the Little Dipper, which is the North Star. (Be sure you are looking at the Northern sky.) The Big Dipper is easy to locate. It is seven bright, clearly visible stars in the shape of a dipper. It is in the constellation called Big Bear or Ursa Major, and it forms the hindquarters and the tail of the bear. Focus your eye on the Big Dipper's bowl and the two stars forming it that are farthest away from the handle. These stars are called pointers; if you follow their line, you will come to the North Star, which is at the tip of the handle of the Little Dipper.

The Little Dipper is in a constellation of stars called Ursa Minor, which forms the Little Bear. You can locate more constellations from this point of reference. Cassiopeia is the queen and looks either like an "M" or a "W" or a little dipper. Cepheus is the king and resembles a house or an A-frame tent. Draco is a dragon or a snake.

When you look up at the sky, take into account that the constellations or groups of stars you are looking for share the sky with other neighboring stars. Prepare yourself to view the entire sky's stars.

Also be aware that the positions of the stars change with the seasons. However, you can see the North Star and the group of constellations nearest to it during the entire year, in varying juxtapositions.

Using the illustration of the Northern Sky in this book, with the current month next to you; hold the paper flat; look up at the northern sky; and although the hour of the evening makes a difference too, you will see the approximate position of the stars.

Use the star locator chart in this book to help you find the exact position of the Big Dipper and Cassiopeia. (Photocopy the two pages of the wheel and cut out the circles as marked.) Place the current month, printed on the smaller wheel, on top of the present time, printed on the larger wheel. Clip the wheels together in that position. Notice the N, S, W, E directions printed above the months and place the wheel in front of you so that the direction you are facing is at the bottom. Now hold the wheel either flat or up in a book-reading position. The stars you see will match up with the stars' positions in the sky. This excellent tool allows you to keep track of the movement of the stars.

Knot Tying

Knot tying makes a productive camping hobby. Advanced knot tying is an excellent preparation for advanced camping. Look for books on knot tying in a library, a bookstore, or a camping store.

CLOVE HITCH - This knot is perfect for tying your hammock, clotheslines, and dining fly. Use a piece of ribbon, rope, or shoestring on a secured pole such as a table leg or chair back.

CLINCH KNOT - Use the clinch knot to tie a hook to a line or leader when you go fishing.

LOOP KNOT - The quick-release loop knot will help to close the drawstrings of your stuff sacks.

BOWLINE KNOT - If you are towing anything, you may need to use a towline. If you choose to use a sturdy rope, the bowline is the best knot.

Nature Study

Recognizing and identifying species that share the outdoors with us is not easy, but the effort is worth it. Whether you are going out in your own backyard or to a vacation spot, there is a great thrill in knowing the names and habits of the species you meet. There is also social value in being able to tell someone exactly what you saw.

When studying nature outside your own property, observe outdoor ethics and/or the law. Do not pick or remove *anything* from the natural environment. Do not attempt to feed the animals. It is not natural for them to eat "served" meals; all wild animals must learn to get their own food, and there is always a chance of getting bitten.

If you are interested in pursuing a nature-related hobby, you will need to get resource material and, in some cases, equipment. Nature classification is dependent on field guides. There are many available for each of the following nature study listings. Publishers who have a line of them include Golden, Audubon, MacMillan, Simon & Schuster, Audubon/Peterson, and the Sierra Club.

Binoculars are good to have for observing and identifying birds and wild animals. Binoculars come with a rating, for instance, 8x21. The 8 is the power of the binoculars—the number of times an object is magnified. A rating of 7 or 8 is recommended. The higher the power, the more limited your field of vision.

The 21 indicates in millimeters the diameter of the front or objective lens—the one farthest away from you and thus closest to the object as you look through the binoculars. It indicates the amount of light admitted into the field of vision—the higher the number, the more light. A diameter of 20 to 50 is recommended.

Use binoculars to view wildlife.

Binoculars that adjust by a single center focusing screw are the most convenient. Practice with the binoculars so that you do not miss some wonderful close-up glimpses of wildlife. First focus your eyes on the object and then lift the binoculars to your eyes without moving your head or your eyes.

A camera just adds to the fun and is a spin-off hobby. Use a 35mm camera, a telephoto lens, and a tripod. To get a picture of birds or wild animals, you must be very quiet and be dressed in clothing that blends with the surroundings. Sometimes you sit quietly in a likely spot and wait.

WILDFLOWER AND TREE IDENTIFICATION - Combine this hobby with a camera and/or a sketch book with colored pencils, and a magnifying glass. It is not within the law nor is it good outdoor manners to pick even a leaf, so you will be glad to have a camera and sketch book. If identification gets too arduous for the occasion, work on it at a more convenient time. The challenge is part of the fun.

In the case of wildflowers, begin by learning the plant families. Each one is grouped according to its common visual characteristics. For example, you can sort out the plants according to the number of petals (from not-apparent, to three, to five, to numerous). Within each of these groups of petal numbers are divisions according to various distinguishing characteristics and habitat, such as location, flower description, type of stem, and many more. Keep in mind that when you see them in your field guide arranged according to color, that is just for convenience. Color actually does not play an important part in the technical classification.

Consider daisy-like flowers, for example. Found all over the country, they are in the *Compositae* or daisy family, which is the largest family of flowering plants. The petals (also called rays) are arranged in a circle around the center disk. The black-eyed Susan, the showy coneflower, and the thin-leaved coneflower are in the Rudbeckia group within the daisy family. They look very much alike, but the leaves are distinguishing characteristics. If the stem and leaves are slightly toothed, it is a black-eyed Susan. If the stem and leaves are coarsely toothed, it is a showy coneflower. And if some of the lower leaves are three lobed, it is a thin-leaved coneflower.

Some trees have distinctive features that identify them at first glance. If you see a tree with acorns, it must be an oak, since all oaks bear acorns and no other trees do. The tulip tree's leaves are unique; in winter it has a candlelike cluster of leaves.

You also can easily spot a pine tree, but that is a family name. There are over sixty species in the pine family. Identifying a species requires looking at identifying characteristics. For example, two of the types of pine are spruce and fir. Look at small twigs that have lost all their needles; if they are rough with projecting stumps, your tree is a spruce. If the twigs are smooth, it is a fir. That narrows it down a bit, and your field guide can help you find out which of the many fir or spruce species it is.

The flower or the fruit of a tree is used in classification. The fruits are divided into berry, drupe, pome, multiple fruit, aggregate fruit, acorn or other nut, key (samara), achene, pod, capsule, or folli- cle. For example, the paired, flat, long-winged fruit on maple trees is a key fruit. This is a good identifying factor for a maple. Getting familiar with these groups would be part of the fun.

The flowering trees are classified by the characteristics of the flower parts, so you need to be familiar with flower parts: petal, pis- til, stigma, style, ovary, stamen, anther, filament, and sepal. All of this terminology is a basis to distinguishing trees from one another and finding out their real name—the species.

INSECT IDENTIFICATION - Insect watching is an interesting hobby. Go to a field or pond; look in flowers and rock or tree crevices; you will find insects practically everywhere. Take a magnifying glass with you, any kind. Look at how the insects move, how they feed, and what they do.

There are around a million distinct species of insects (100,000 of them live in North America), and more to be discovered. Just learn- ing some basic classes and orders of insects helps you sort out what you are observing. They are grouped according to habitat and their general appearance (size, shape, and color) as well as basic physical characteristics, such as placement of wings, shape of body, shape of head, type of abdomen, and type of mouth. It can get very confusing, but a field guide helps clarify the different groups. ·

To add to the confusion, many people label almost any small creature with more than four legs as an insect. Some very small crea- tures are not insects at all. Similarly, many people call these little creatures bugs, but bugs are only some of the insects known. Consider the sow bug (pill bug), for example. It is not an insect or bug at all. It is a crustacean, of which there are two major groups. The sow bug is in the *Malacostraca* group. Most members of this group are marine. The sow bug, being a relative, likes dampness. Look under stones or bark where it is moist or dark, and you are likely to find a sow bug. Just remember, it is not an insect.

BIRD IDENTIFICATION - If you have enjoyed watching birds at home around a bird feeder, you have begun to develop some background skills to get you going on a camping trip. Begin by looking at basic shapes; your binoculars will be useful here. Ask yourself some questions about the bird's size in relation to others in the vicinity; shape in terms of round, long, short, stubby, slim; color of the bill; length of the tail; wing description, short, straight, curved; and identifying features of the feathers, color, rings, stripes.

Learning to identify bird types by shape is the first basic information to grasp. This practice will get you started on keen observation of bird parts and the use of correct terminology, both necessary skills for leading you to the right page in your field guide.

The goal is to identify the name of the species. After mastering the basic shape, focus your attention on the bird's head; this part alone is usually enough for the experts. They observe the shape and color of the bill and its length relative to the head; eye markings such as a dark line through the eye, a light stripe over the eye, or a pale ring around the eye. They also study the intensity of all of these markings. They observe the crown (top of head), color of the throat, and other distinctive markings.

For example, a bird often seen by campers is the jay bird, because it will eat anything and finds good pickings in campgrounds

The Steller's jay

(thus the nickname "camp robber"). There are about eight jay species in North America. "Jay" comes from the Latin *gaius* or *gaia*, meaning noisy or chattering. The blue jay is common in the Eastern United States and Central Canada, and the Steller's jay is common in the Western United States. The blue jay has a white breast and belly, and the Steller's jay has a charcoal breast with a light blue belly. The head of the blue jay has detailed markings, including an eye line, in blue, black, and white. The head of the Steller's jay is solid charcoal with a white line on the forehead, white lines on the chin, and a white eye stripe.

People who talk a great deal or move around all of the time cannot be good bird watchers. You must be quiet and move carefully and have patience. Birds are shy.

WILD ANIMAL IDENTIFICATION - On a camping trip you may see or hear some wild animals. Learn some of their basic characteristics and how to identify them so you can share your knowledge with your family. You may hear, for instance, some yapping at night somewhere in the distance. It is possibly a coyote, but because of its secretive nature you probably never will see one. Other animals that you might see, find tracks from, or discover have been in your food or garbage at night are described below.

• Ground squirrel and chipmunk. It is easy to confuse the ground squirrel with the chipmunk but not when you know the trick. The chipmunk has facial stripes, and the ground squirrel does not. The golden-mantled ground squirrel is most easily confused with the

Golden-mantled ground squirrel

chipmunk, because it has stripes that run along the top of the head, a ring of white fur circling the eyes, and thirteen whitish stripes with spaces interrupting some of them along the back. The chipmunk always has stripes running along its body. Both the chipmunk and the ground squirrel are in the same family *(Sciuridae)*, which means "shade tail."

When you are camping, it is fascinating and fun to watch ground squirrels and chipmunks sit up, eat swiftly and continuously, and soak up sun on a log or stump while watching for enemies and surveying their domain. Chipmunks and some ground squirrels have large, internal cheek pouches. When their cheeks are bulged, they are carrying nuts and seeds. Most of them burrow in a limb or underground for a habitat. Sometimes they can become a nuisance when they are too numerous and too friendly. They may get into boxes or bags of food at your campsite during the daytime, so be careful to close up everything.

• Skunk. There are four species of skunk: the striped (two white stripes down the back); the hog-nosed (one broad white stripe down the back); the spotted (series of white stripes that are broken up and appear as white spots); and the hooded (all white top with a small black patch in the middle and a very fluffy white tail). All have glossy black coats. The striped skunk is about the size of a plump housecat. All of the species are found throughout the United States.

Skunks are not good fighters, but they have good defense. When disturbed, a skunk goes through an elaborate aggressive display. It flaunts its conspicuous markings as a warning to predators to back off. It also can emit a powerful odor, discharged accurately to a distance of ten to twelve feet. Because the skunk sleeps during the day, it usually does not bother people, but you might see one in your garbage or food boxes at night if they are not put away.

• Raccoon. The raccoon is easily identified by the black mask on its face and its ringed (black-banded) furry tail. It has a stocky build. It is an intelligent, plucky, and clever animal. It fingers its food before eating to sort it and tear it, wetting its paws to enhance the sense of touch.

The raccoon is found in almost the entire United States. It is primarily nocturnal. It is not unusual, however, to see it in the morning or early in the evening, when it wanders through campgrounds looking for food. It has nimble fingers and can get into a closed cupboard easily unless it is properly latched. It also can climb into garbage cans. Remember to keep your food or garbage in the campground's latched cupboard or your car at night.

• Deer. The three most common deer are the mule deer, the black-tailed (a subspecies of the mule deer), and the white-tailed. The white-tailed deer is found in many states (usually not in California, Nevada, or Utah), but the black-tailed deer and mule deer are found in the western half of the country. The mule deer and black-tailed deer are more likely to be found in unpopulated areas in higher elevations, while the white-tailed deer is found in farmland, brushy areas, and woods.

Male whitetail deer

Knowing the difference between these three deer is interesting if you will be doing some hiking when you go camping. If you see a deer, usually it is a doe, because bucks tend to stay in heavy cover. You are looking at a mule deer if the ears are rather large. The buck's antlers are one main branch coming up vertically out of the head with points that each have another point, forming a fork.

You are looking at a white-tailed deer if the antlers' main branch has only single points. (It is interesting to note that, whatever the species, the size of the antlers and the number of spikes are determined by his diet.) The white-tailed deer gets its name from the white underside of its twelve-inch–long tail, which is displayed like a flag when the deer is alarmed or dashes off. The top of the tail is brown with a white edge. The tail of the black-tailed deer is blackish or brown.

The deer is color blind and does not have good vision for shapes. If you want to get close to a deer, you have a good chance if you are quiet and move very slowly, as it is quick to catch motion.

The black bear

• Black bear. This bear may be really black or any shade of brown, from yellowish and silvery to reddish cinnamon. It is distinguished from the grizzly by its pointed face and straight profile and the absence of a hump on its shoulders. It also climbs trees. (The brown and grizzly bears are technically considered subspecies of the same species. The black bear and the grizzly do not live in the same location, so locality is a good guide for establishing which one you are observing.)

The black bear is adaptable and intelligent. It quickly learns to utilize people's garbage for food and to solicit handouts from tourists in the national parks. Remember that it is dangerous to feed a bear. It likes apple pie, chocolate cake, and applesauce (the black bear has a sweet tooth). If refused, it may take these by force. It tears open tin cans and goes off with sugar, flour, hams, and bacon. Lock up your food at night.

With leisure and opportunity it becomes very sociable. It will clown and squint up its eyes with pleasure when admired. But it is powerful and potentially dangerous, despite its seemingly comic antics. It can claw, wound, and kill. The black bear lives throughout the United States.

• Grizzly bear. The grizzly's color ranges from blond to black, but frequently it has dark brown with silver-tipped guard hairs on the upper body, which give the animal a "grizzled" or frosty appearance. (See the photograph next page) It is distinguished from the black bear by the fact that it does not climb trees (except for a few rare observed instances); it is larger and heavier (on the average); it has a blunter head, a dished (round) face with a forehead that is slightly more raised (the head profile appears shorter and less slender); it has a hump on its shoulders; and it is more ferocious.

The grizzly has great strength and an aggressive intelligence. When confronted, it fights instead of fleeing. A grizzly does not like to be surprised. Hikers in bear country should make noise or even wear a "bear bell." If you are close to one without a tree to climb, play dead, curled up with your head down to protect the vital parts

151

The grizzly bear

of your body, in case the bear tries to tousle you. This bear has a keen attraction to the odor of food—even that which is left on clothes. Both magnificent and terrible, the grizzly will never change its ways to accommodate mankind.

The grizzly is found in two of the national parks where you might go camping—Glacier and Yellowstone. It lives in Wyoming, Montana, and Idaho. The brown bear lives in Alaska.

Learning About Maps

At a campground, it is fun and helpful to have a map of the area showing the location of the local places of interest. If you enjoy simple hikes, a hiking trail map will prove to be useful; often the campground has these available. These maps are fairly easy to read, and using a compass with them adds another skill.

A map of interest to serious hikers is a topographic map. These maps differ from ordinary maps in that they show the physical terrain and elevations of the land. An ordinary hiking map shows lakes, rivers, roads and trails in simple detail and gives a general idea of mountains and valleys. A topographic map gives more information. It gives the detail of mountains and valleys, letting the hiker know the easiest places to hike. Someday you may want to hike into desolate areas. Learning to read a topographic map now would be an interesting hobby and an excellent skill that can be applied when you are ready for advanced camping.

A topographic map by the U.S. Geological Survey enlarges up to an area of six by nine miles on one sheet of paper. Sometimes you need more than one map to cover an area of interest. The best way to get a topographic map is to write for a catalog of the state you are interested in, which will show you all the available maps of the state. For maps of areas east of the Mississippi River, including Minnesota, write: Eastern Distribution Branch, U.S. Geological Survey, 1200 South Eads Street, Arlington, VA 22202.

To order maps of areas west of the Mississippi River, including Alaska and Louisiana, write: Western Distribution Branch, U.S. Geological Survey, Box 25286, Federal Center, Building 41, Denver, CO 80225. If your order combines both of these areas, it may be placed with either office.

For Canada, write: Map Distribution Office, 615 Booth Street, Ottawa, Ontario, Canada K1A 0E9.

The U.S. Geological Survey also has a central information source where you can write for answers to any map-related questions that you have. Write: National Cartographic Information Center, 507 National Center, Reston, VA 22092.

PHYSICAL RECREATION AND DIVERSIONS

Most people go camping to do something more than camp and pursue a hobby. Even an avid photographer combines hiking with picture taking. The possibilities are many.

If you decide to go hiking, bicycling, or boating or pursue any other outdoor recreation for half a day or so, there are certain basic items you should take. They are:

• Food and water

- Hat
- Clothes for layering according to the weather
- Sunscreen
- Sunglasses
- First-aid kit

A camera and a pair of binoculars always would be fun to have along.

Hiking

Take advantage of the trails in the area. Enjoy nature and the physical exercise with your family at your side.

Hikers vary in their physical stamina and their style of hiking. Some like to dawdle, and some like to make good time. When a family goes hiking, everyone should adjust his pace to the youngest or slowest walker. Hiking with toddlers presents more problems than hiking with children of any other age group because they are heavy to carry, and they are slow walkers.

Babies and small toddlers can ride in backpack baby carriers,

Enjoy hiking the trails in your area.

which come in luxurious new designs. Shop around for the one you like. Observe safety precautions while using a carrier. Never bend forward at the waist. Use a safety strap and fasten the child in securely. Be on guard for low branches that could brush across the child's face. Check the child for chafing. See to it that the child's eyes and skin are protected from bright sun.

HIKING SHOES AND SOCKS - For hiking, you should have either a pair of walking shoes, trail shoes, or hiking boots. It is impossible to categorize these shoes accurately because they overlap, and different sources use different terms. When trying them on it is important to have an idea of the market, a definite idea of how long and where you will be hiking, and a good choice of socks, and maybe insoles.

Hiking boots are designed for hard and steady use and are for advanced campers. They are best for winter backpacking, sloshing through streams, overnight hikes, and when carrying packs over fifty pounds. For moderate loads and moderate trails, use a lighter shoe. The first rule is to avoid getting too much shoe, and the second rule is to get enough shoe. The terrain you travel, your weight, the average weight of your pack, and the feel that you prefer will help you determine the proper shoe. Choose a shoe no heavier than you need because lightweight shoes are easier on the wear and tear of trails and paths.

Never go on a long hike in new boots. Break them in first. Wear them indoors for a few hours, so you can return them if they are uncomfortable. If you feel pressure points of excessive rubbing, return the boots.

Most hikers wear at least two pairs of socks to provide insulation and padding. The socks rub against each other, reducing friction and protecting the feet from blisters. For less strenuous activities and in the heat, some prefer just one pair of properly fitting socks.

Your choice of the fabric content depends on the shoes or boots being worn, the weather, and personal preference. You get to know your own feet, and choose what is right for your needs out of a myriad of combinations: thickness of each sock, amount of socks (from one to three), and various fabrics and blends. Insoles are yet another option, as they can be used to fill out the boot when your preference is one or two thin pairs of socks. Work with the combinations to make yourself comfortable.

Wool is a popular fabric for socks because it insulates, absorbs sweat, and is warm when wet; however, it itches and is not durable. Top-grade, all-wool socks make a good outer sock. They are warm in winter and cool in summer. Wool blends and nylon heel and toe reinforcement are good.

Cotton is soft against the skin, and it absorbs sweat. It is popular in the summer when the dampness does not matter and the lack of warmth is an advantage. Cotton or silk liners are popular in the summer.

Polypropylene fibers do not hold moisture; they pass it out to the outer sock, keeping your feet dry. A mixture of olefin (seventy percent) and nylon (ten percent) is popular as a wick-dry summer sock, because it keeps the foot dry in hot weather. Silk and nylon are popular inner socks for the feel and for hot spots on the foot that could lead to blisters.

Hikers always take extra socks for anything longer than half a day because the socks get wet. They usually change them during the noon rest stop when it is advisable to take off the boots for a while anyway. Adding a pair of socks for downhill hiking tightens the fit and avoids blisters. Shedding a pair or changing into lighter socks helps when the feet swell from hiking. Change into dry socks after a day of hiking to avoid dampness and chilling.

STRETCHING - Consider your physical fitness before embarking on a hike. If you do something aerobic on a regular weekly basis, you are physically fit. Awareness of your own body is the key. Be in condition, and be sure to do some stretches at the campsite before your hike.

Stretching strengthens the muscles that are not used when walking, as well as those that are. Stretching before hiking loosens muscles for a longer stride and prepares them for activity. Stretching after a hike compensates for the tightening effect that occurs naturally as a result of vigorous muscle use and prevents muscle imbalance injuries and soreness.

Always stretch slowly, smoothly, and painlessly. Let the muscle stretch itself. Extend the muscle to where you feel it stretching, then hold it there for a short count, whatever feels right to you. Keep breathing. Never bounce; bouncing only tightens the muscles. Here are four basic stretches.

• Achilles and calf stretch. The Achilles tendon is located directly behind each ankle.

This movement stretches parts of the leg used in the toe-off phase of the walking cycle. With the back knee slightly bent, you concentrate on the Achilles tendon. With the back knee straight, you concentrate on the calf.

Grasp a tree or lean against a wall or car. Keeping your feet pointing straight ahead, move one leg back and the other toward the tree. Slowly stretch the back heel down, and slightly bend the back knee. Switch.

Repeat, keeping the back knee straight.

• Standing hamstring stretch. The hamstring is the large muscle directly behind the thigh.

This movement stretches the muscles throughout the back of the thighs, which tend to tighten during long walks.

Stand in front of a picnic table, car, or railing—a sturdy object of a height that is comfortable for your height and flexibility. You want your leg to come up to just enough height for a comfortable stretch. Lift one foot onto the table and hold. Position yourself far enough from the table so that just your foot rests on the table. Switch legs and repeat.

• Quadricep stretch. The quadricep is the large muscle in front of the thigh.

This movement is excellent for the front thigh, which stabilizes the knees and lifts the legs during the swinging phase of the walking cycle.

Stand erect near something or someone for balance, if needed. Raise one leg in back of you and grasp its ankle with the hand on the same side. The other hand is free for balance and hold. Switch.

• Groin stretch. The groin muscle is located where the thigh joins the abdomen.

This movement stretches the groin, the inner thigh, the abdominal, and the chest areas.

Stand tall, keeping your back and hips straight. Lunge forward until your forward knee is above your toes. Raise your arms overhead for balance and hold. Switch.

WHAT TO TAKE - For any hike lasting about a half day, you will want to take the basic items listed previously. For longer hikes or wilderness hikes, other important items are:

• Compass
• Clothing, for all possible weather conditions
• Extra food
• Flashlight
• Fire starter (candle)
• Pocketknife
• Matches in waterproof container
• Toilet paper
• Swimsuit and towel (optional)
• Plastic bags for garbage

HIKING SKILLS - There are four main hiking topics that all hikers, beginner or advanced, should know—how to have a low impact on nature, treatment of drinking water, safety when lost, and environmental interest group participation.

• Low impact on nature. Preserving nature should be an attitude— your own feeling and integrity about keeping the land in a state of natural beauty. Every region presents a different emphasis on preservation based on what there is to maintain and the region's problems. Be aware of the concerns in your hiking area.

Trying to protect and preserve the land (nature) at the same time that it is being used is a severe problem. So-called wilderness areas are marred with black fire spots, polluted water, trampled vegetation, sunken and eroded trails, and stripped trees. Here is how we must react. Use water 100 feet away from its source. Stay on trails and wear lightweight shoes that do not cut into the trails. Do not litter, and pack out all of your garbage. Leave pets at home. Never remove a living thing from the landscape.

• Water purification. First of all, do not add to polluted water by using it at the source (river, stream, lake). Take the water 100 feet away from the source. Do not get into the water with a dirty body.

The waters have become polluted, and you should not drink or brush your teeth with it. Giardia may exist in a crystal-clear and free-running stream. It is the most common bacterial disease that is transmitted through water contaminated by human or animal waste. You would spoil your trip with a case of dysentery—diarrhea, gas, cramps, fever.

Purify the water with the following methods. Boil water from one to thirty minutes, depending on the clarity and the source. Boil longer at altitudes of 2,000 feet and above. For example, at 7,000 feet, boil water fifteen to forty-five minutes. Purchase water purification tablets at a camping supply store; use them according to the manufacturer's instructions. Note how long the tablets are still effective after the package is opened, and look for brands that state they are effective against giardia.

• Safety for the lost. Casual hikers who wander from the trails risk getting lost. Know what to do and teach the procedure to those in your hiking group. Your children should wear a whistle and know how to use it.

Concentrate on direction. Do not shift position unless you are quite sure of what you are doing. If you do move, leave a note or

159

mark the place with stones or sticks in groups of three, which indicates "help." Show the direction you have taken by making trail arrows out of stones, brush, or twigs.

Climb a tree to find landmarks. Try to sort out where you are.

Blow your whistle. Three signals of any kind is a distress signal. Two is a response signal.

In the case of an adult, and when things look serious, nothing attracts the interest of the authorities as quickly as smoke. Be safe. Make a small fire out of green wood, which will produce a lot of smoke. Try to keep warm, sheltered, and supplied with water. If it gets dark, do not wander around. Wait until morning to find your way. Instruct children to stay put, no matter what.

• Environmental interest group participation. Be in touch with the National Trails Coalition. You may want to take a part in their efforts. Write: The National Trails Coalition, c/o American Hiking Society, 1015 31st Street Northwest, Washington, D.C. 20007. Or call 1-202-385-3252.

Bicycling

Taking along a bicycle for every family member can be a priority on a camping trip. Bicycling provides exercise, sightseeing transportation, and campground transportation.

Bicycles allow family members to explore the surrounding areas at their own pace.

If your sightseeing takes a half a day or more, you should consider taking a small pump, lock and cable, tube patch kit, lights, reflectors, a quarter for a pay phone, plus the basic items listed previously.

Safety is important when bicycling. Observe the advice of the experts and **wear a helmet**. Do not be deceived by the notion that you are in a rural area where a car is not likely to hit you. First of all, there are bicycle crossings in camp areas where the roads are busy. Also, you can fall off your bicycle if a dog or another cyclist gets in your way, or if a rock or crack in the terrain throws you off balance. Get a helmet that fits snugly. Even though the hard-shell helmets are heavier, they are better protection than wearing a soft-shell helmet. Remember to ride with the traffic, *not* against the traffic. Obey all road signs and traffic laws.

If you are carrying a young child on your bicycle, he should be in a good-quality child's seat, wearing a child-size helmet.

Boating

Good boats for a camping trip are ones that are paddled or rowed—a kayak, canoe, rowboat, or inflatable boat. All share some worthwhile advantages—they are portable and invigorating and provide transportation, fun, and challenge. Campers love being able to take them into remote areas. They can go to better spots for swimming, sunning, reading, sleeping, walking, sketching, bird watching, and taking pictures.

You might want to begin with an inflatable boat for the first few trips. These are easy to take along, not very expensive to buy, and can provide a satisfying and enjoyable experience. Later you might want to invest in a different boat, or you can try renting one near your camping area.

Whichever type of boat you use, you must have paddles and life preservers (PFDs) on board. The stern paddler can use a paddle about chin height, and the bow paddler use one about six inches shorter. The life preserver has to be the right size for comfort and safety. Your PFD should keep you in a semivertical position in the water, provide protection from the rocks, and not be a hindrance when you are swimming.

Boaters should always have foreknowledge of the waters they will be paddling. They must be aware of weather conditions that might agitate the water as well as temperature changes that would be too cold for the body.

Fishing

Fishing is a popular recreation for all ages. And besides being fun to do, it also may provide some food for supper or even breakfast.

You do not need a license to fish in the ocean unless either you are fishing for salmon or you are on a public pier. But you do need a license to fish in inland waters. Contact your state fish and game department about regulations.

Choose your fishing style according to the kinds of fish you are likely to catch. Each species has its own habits and average weight. You can ask about local fishing when you are in a particular area. If you first want to test out the sport or introduce your small child to the joys of fishing, it is possible to do some still-fishing with a hand-held line.

For still-fishing you need about fifty to 100 feet of drop line wound around a frame, and a sinker on the end of the line. Or, use a ten- to twelve-foot pole and a line of the same length with a cork float (bobber) instead of a sinker. For both methods, choose a hook that is sized according to the fish you expect to catch and tie it to the line using a clinch knot. Use live bait—worms, minnows, frogs, crayfish, grasshoppers, crickets, caterpillars, and other insects and bugs. Drop the line in the water and wait.

Most people want to use all-purpose tackle (rod and reel) in the small streams and lakes around the camping area. Ask locally about the most effective bait. Knowledge about the four most common freshwater fishing styles (all using different tackle) will help your shopping.

BAIT CASTING - This technique is a little tricky. The reel is positioned with the winding of the line running parallel to the rod. Since the reel spins as the line unwinds from it during the cast, you must stop it with your thumb on the spool at just the right time. You make the cast (throw the line out) by flipping the rod forward, sending the lure out, which unwinds the line as it goes. When the lure loses forward momentum and stops, the reel will keep spinning and the line will tangle if you do not stop it.

SPIN CASTING - This technique is the easiest to learn because you do not have to stop the reel. The reel is in a fixed spool position, which is placed on the rod with the wound thread lines running perpendicular to the rod. After bringing the rod up and back with a fast snappy throw, you start the cast on the reel by releasing your thumb from a lever on the reel.

SPINNING - The spinning technique also uses the fixed spool principle, but the spool is open and mounted under the rod, and the crank is turned with the left hand to return the slack in the line after it hits the water. (In spincasting the spool has a hood, the spool is mounted on top of the rod, and the crank is turned with the right hand.)

FLY-FISHING - Fly fishing requires artificial flies for bait. Sometimes they float on top of the water, and sometimes they go under the water. The fly line is much heavier than the ordinary bait-casting line or spin-casting monofilament line because the weight of the line carries the weightless fly out. You use a leader (thin line or monofilament) to attach the hook to the line so that fish do not see the line. The purpose of the reel is just to store the line.

Fishermen consider fly fishing the highest form of sport fishing because they interact with the fish. When the conditions are right, fly fishing is more fun than anything else. But it takes practice. Since it is an art, too, you cannot learn it in a paragraph. However, no one should be afraid to try it; it is not that difficult.

The cast is divided into the front cast and the back cast. For these instructions: Think of a clock over your head with twelve o'clock at the top of your head, two o'clock in front of you, and eleven o'clock in back of you. Begin with the back cast. Holding the rod with the thumb on top and the wrist joint cocked down, point the rod in the two o'clock position. With your free hand at waist level, hold the line or anchor it under your thumb. Now accelerate the rod briskly to the twelve o'clock position. Then, with a flick of the wrist backwards, accelerate the rod briskly to the eleven o'clock position. When you feel the tip of the rod flex under the pull of the line straightening behind, you begin the forward cast. Still holding the line firmly in the free hand, cock the wrist joint backwards. Briskly accelerate the rod forward by flicking it. Stop abruptly at the two o'clock position. This sets the line streaming forwards, tugging at the rod tip. Now release the line you have been holding with your spare hand and follow through with the rod as the line falls to the surface.

Have a good time fishing, and abide by good sportsmanship. Obey all fishing laws. Be careful of other anglers (fishermen) near you when you are casting and make sure no one is behind you. Avoid crowding. The first angler on the spot has priority. If your line tangles with another angler's line, do not blame him even if it is his fault. Throw back the small fish and give them a chance to grow for a better catch later on. Keep the hook stuck into a cork when you are not using it. Do not leave spare hooks lying around. Cut the hook from the line when finished and store it in a box. Know what to do if someone gets hurt. Leave your fishing spot cleaner than you found it.

Swimming

One of the highlights of a summertime camping trip is often the proximity of a lake or ocean for swimming at all times of the day. It is important, however, that you know how to swim or to stay afloat. Observe the following safety tips:

• Make sure someone is watching you or swimming with you

• Adapt to cool or cold water slowly

• Do not swim when you are overheated, overtired, or after eating a meal

• Beware of unfamiliar swimming areas (*know* that a place is safe)

• Always know the depth when diving

• Do not overjudge your distance ability

• Do not stay underwater so long that you take chances

• Be aware of the safety of others

• Do not *depend* on water wings or other such contraptions for the safety of children

Panning for Gold

Check the library for maps showing gold-country areas. Look for a dry, half dry, or full creek, river, or stream bed that is below 4,000 feet in California, Nevada, Washington, Oregon, Kentucky, Tennessee, or Colorado.

Gold panning is a lot of fun. Take along a metal pie pan for each person. Go to a creek, stream, or river site that is known to have gold. Fill the pan with either wet or dry rock, gravel, sand, or a combination. Take the pan and debris to the water and fill it with water. Swish it all around and around. Look at the bottom for a settling of black sand and gold.

Night Life Underwater

If you have access to a lake and a dock, you can observe fish at night. You will need a waterproof flashlight and ten feet of strong twine. Tie the twine to the flashlight. Use tight, secure knots, and fashion it so the light will lay flat in the water. You might want to use a series of wraps and knots along the light and have a ten-foot length come from each end for balance. How ever you design it, the point is not to lose your flashlight.

After dark, turn the light on and lower it off a dock or from a boat into six to eight feet of clear water. Turn the light slowly by twisting the line. The light will attract fish, and you can see them in the light beam. Do not even pretend you are fishing; night fishing with a light is usually prohibited.

10

Breaking up Camp and Preserving Memories

The vacation is almost over; what is left is three to six hours of taking down the camp—depending on how long you stayed and how many people were in your camp. Is this small, final segment of your vacation just work or is it another opportunity to be outdoors with your family?

Is the vacation over? What about the memories? They will weave into your life, building stronger relationships and stronger individual personalities. The physical exertion and rest, and the mental rest and refreshment provide strength and quality to the days ahead. The education provided by nature-related hobbies enriches your daily activities.

BREAKING UP CAMP

Just like setting up camp, the responsibility of breaking up camp belongs to the group. It is a time for the family to work in unison and, after everything is packed, to share a sense of triumph. It means working together, sharing tasks, avoiding rush and harassment, providing time for refreshment and repose, and maintaining an upbeat attitude.

Develop a routine. Gather all soiled laundry into laundry bags and pack according to your personal preference. Sort the food—nibbling while packing—into car snacks and a light meal to eat before leaving. Also sort out the items that would be handy in the car while driving home—the camp file; magazines, books, car games, and toys; pillows and blankets; tissue; first-aid kit; flashlight; and layering items of clothing.

Take pride in how you care for your equipment and how you leave your campsite. Sweep out the tent thoroughly and fold it up carefully. Air out all of the sleeping bags before packing. Take care that all the equipment is clean, packaged, and protected; for example, the stove should be wiped, the lantern glass should be protected, and the clothesline and clothespins can be packed conveniently in a bag together.

Leave Your Campsite Spotless

Just before you go home, plan to have a competitive pick-up game. After you are all packed and ready to go home, have the children pick up debris around your campsite. Set up a time limit (about fifteen minutes) and definite boundaries. Make the fire pit and the grill stove out-of-bounds. Instruct the children to display their collection of garbage (bits of foil and plastic, peelings, bottle caps, whatever) on individual pieces of paper that are set up on the picnic table, so the parents, who are the judges, do not know who collected which pile. Judge the findings for amount, keeping in mind that bulky items look like more. Give a prize to all. If you planned ahead, you can have gum, tablets, or souvenirs ready, if not, give money. The purpose of this game is excellent—Leave the Campsite Spotless.

Because the preservation of the natural scenery is a priority with true campers, the who-can-pick-up-the-most-litter game can also be played while you walk along paths and trails. Again, it is nice to have a prize.

Above all do not let this last segment of your vacation ruin the idyllic stay you have had. Careful planning, cooperation, and a relaxed, positive attitude can make breaking up camp a highlight of the vacation. Let that be your goal.

UNPACKING AND EQUIPMENT MAINTENANCE

You are glad to be home, you are tired, and all at once everything has to be done. It is overwhelming—plants, pets, mail, telephone messages, and a car full of gear, dirty laundry, and kids with minds of their own.

This phase defies the possibility of fun and recreation. But take on the challenge. At the right time, in the right tone, ask everyone to take a part. Ideally, you have planned for and allowed some time for this task. If too much putting away and catching up is allotted too little time, adjust your expectations and save some personality and energy for pleasantries.

Pack your camping gear carefully, and you will add to its life. Basically the rule is to keep everything clean and dry. Air out the sleeping bags and store them over hangers in your closets. Replace the fuel your gear requires so that you are ready for a trip on a minute's notice. Turn the tent inside out to shake out any remaining dirt, turn it back, check for spots that require sponging, rinse, let dry, fold, and put away. Store your ice chest(s) with the lids unfastened. This will allow circulation and save on the sealing. Wash off all of the dirt from your hatchet, shovel, saw, and camp knife. Dirt on steel attracts moisture from the air, which causes rust. Dry and sharpen the hatchet and knife. You can lightly oil the metal of these tools.

PRESERVING MEMORIES

Preserving memories can begin on the way home, while your vacation is fresh in everyone's mind. Together, go over the highlights and meaningful moments. Or, if others would prefer to sleep or talk about something different, use this time to take your own personal inventory. This is not a time for critical evaluation—you are still on vacation. But it is a time to sort out what was good. Capture in your mind those very special things that are so abundant in a camping vacation—a time by the campfire, sunning at a scenic spot, an evening walk around the camping area, and congregating at the picnic table over a crossword puzzle.

169

Focus on the interdependence your family has shared as well as the independent times you have experienced. Maybe setting up the tent was rich in cooperation and teaching. Perhaps one of the children learned to swim. Maybe your teenager's attempt at some special camp cooking was a big hit. Take this time to appreciate your family. Be grateful to the children for their desire to please and their glee. Praise the person who organized the hundreds of details that go into packing.

If you or your teenager has been keeping a log of the trip, this may be a good time to record trip highlights, calamities, quotes, and experiences. Include feelings and reactions, not just travel facts. Keep it light and fun.

Memories come flooding back as you unpack and see your souvenirs again. And when the photographs of the trip have been developed, you will vividly remember it all over again. This is another time for sharing and family bonding. You and your family have experienced something special together, away from the structure that presses in on life at home.

Then put it all together in a family meeting with, perhaps, someone taking more notes in the trip diary. Now is the time for sharing thoughts about where it could have gone better. You will hear about the length of the drive, the cold oatmeal, the heat, and other personal gripes. Use this meeting as an evaluation to be used as a guideline for the next trip.

There will be a next trip, of course. You opened the door to fulfillment by going camping. You'll keep it open.

Appendix

CAMPSITE INFORMATION

State Parks

A letter to the states that you are interested in will bring you a reservation form and a packet of materials. Usually you get a very nice guide to all of the state parks with their addresses and telephone numbers. When you write the specific parks, you get detailed information.

Alabama Department of Conservation and Natural Resources
Division of State Parks
64 North Union Street, Montgomery, AL 36130
205-261-3334

Alaska Division of Parks and Outdoor Recreation
Department of Natural Resources
3601 C Street, P.O. Box 107001, Anchorage, AK 99510
907-762-2600

Arizona State Parks
800 West Washington, Suite 415, Phoenix, AZ 85007
602-542-4174

Arkansas State Parks
One Capitol Mall, Little Rock, AR 72201
501-371-7743

California Department of Parks and Recreation
P.O. Box 942896, Sacramento, CA 94296-0001
916-445-2358

Colorado Department of Natural Resources
Division of Parks and Outdoor Recreation
1313 Sherman Street, Room 618, Denver, CO 80203
303-866-2884

Connecticut Department of Environmental Protection
Office of State Parks and Recreation
Division of Conservation and Preservation
165 Capitol Avenue, Hartford, CT 060106
203-566-2304

Delaware Department of Natural Resources and Environmental Control
Division of Parks and Recreation
89 Kings Highway, P.O. Box 1401, Dover, DE 19903
302-736-4401

Florida Department of Natural Resources
Division of Recreation and Parks
3900 Commonwealth Boulevard, Tallahassee, FL 32399
904-488-6131

Georgia Department of Natural Resources
Parks, Recreation and Historic Sites Division
205 Butler Street Southeast, Suite 1352, Atlanta, GA 30334
404-656-2753

Hawaii Department of Land and Natural Resources
Division of State Parks, Outdoor Recreation and Historic Sites
P.O. Box 621, Honolulu, HI 96809
808-548-7455

Idaho Department of Parks and Recreation
Statehouse Mall, Boise, ID 83720
208-334-2154

Illinois Department of Conservation
Division of Land Management
600 North Grand Avenue West, Springfield, IL 62701
217-782-1395

Indiana Department of Natural Resources
Division of State Parks
616 State Office Building, Indianapolis, IN 46204
317-232-4136

Iowa Department of Natural Resources
Bureau of State Parks Management
Wallace State Office Building, Des Moines, IA 50319-0034
515-281-5886

Kansas Department of Wildlife and Parks
Landon State Office Building
900 Jackson Street, Suite 502, Topeka, KS 66612
913-296-2281

Kentucky Department of Parks
Capital Plaza Towers, 10th Floor, Frankfort, KY 40601
502-564-2172

Louisiana Department of Culture, Recreation and Tourism
Office of State Parks
P.O. Drawer 44426, Baton Rouge, LA 70804-4426
504-342-8111

Maine Department of Conservation
Bureau of Parks and Recreation
Statehouse Station #22, Augusta, ME 04333
207-289-3821

Maryland Department of Natural Resources
Forest and Park Operations
Tawes State Office Building
580 Taylor Avenue, Annapolis, MD 21401
301-974-3771

Massachusetts Department of Environmental Management
Division of Forests and Parks
Leverett Saltonstall Building, 100 Cambridge Street, Boston, MA 02202
617-727-3180

Michigan Department of Natural Resources
Parks Division
P.O. Box 30028, Lansing, MI 48909
517-373-1270

Minnesota Department of Natural Resources
Division of Parks and Recreation
500 Lafayette Road, St. Paul, MN 55155-4039
612-296-2270

Mississippi Department of Natural Resources
Bureau of Recreation and Parks
P.O. Box 10600, Jackson, MS 39209
601-961-5240

Missouri Department of Natural Resources
Division of Parks, Recreation and Historic Preservation
P.O. Box 176, Jefferson City, MO 65102
314-751-9392

Montana Department of Fish, Wildlife and Parks
Parks Division
Capitol Station, Helena, MT 59620
406-444-3750

Nebraska Game and Parks Commission
P.O. Box 30370, Lincoln, NE 68503
402-471-0641

Nevada Department of Conservation and Natural Resources
Division of State Parks
201 South Fall Street, Room 119, Capitol Complex,
Carson City, NV 89710
702-885-4370

New Hampshire Department of Resources and Economic Development
Division of Parks and Recreation
P.O. Box 856, Concord, NH 03301
603-271-3255

New Jersey Department of Environmental Protection
Division of Parks and Forestry
CN 404, 501 East State Street, Trenton, NJ 08625
609-292-2733

New Mexico State Park and Recreation Division
Energy, Minerals and Natural Resources Department
408 Galisteo Street, Villagra Building, Santa Fe, NM 87503-1147
505-827-7465

New York Office of Parks, Recreation and Historic Preservation
Agency Building No. 1, Empire State Plaza, Albany, NY 12238
518-474-0463

**North Carolina Department of Natural Resources
and Community Development**
Division of Parks and Recreation
P.O. Box 27687, Raleigh, NC 27611-7687
919-733-4181

North Dakota Parks and Recreation Department
1424 West Century Avenue, Suite 202, Bismarck, ND 58501
701-224-4887

Ohio Department of Natural Resources
Division of Parks and Recreation
Fountain Square, C-3, Columbus, OH 43224
614-265-6511

Oklahoma Tourism and Recreation Department
Division of State Parks
500 Will Rogers Building, Oklahoma City, OK 73105
405-521-3411

Oregon Department of Transportation
State Parks and Recreation Division
525 Trade Street, Southeast, Room 301, Salem, OR 97310
503-378-5019

Pennsylvania Department of Environmental Resources
Bureau of State Parks
2150 Herr Street, Harrisburg, PA 17103-1625
717-787-6640

Rhode Island Department of Environmental Management
Division of Parks and Recreation
22 Hayes Street, Providence, RI 02908
401-277-2632

South Carolina Department of Parks, Recreation and Tourism
Division of State Parks
Edgar A. Brown Building, 1205 Pendleton Street
Columbia, SC 29201
803-734-0159

South Dakota Department of Game, Fish and Parks
Division of Parks and Recreation
Sigurd Anderson Building, 445 East Capitol Avenue
Pierre, SD 57501
605-773-3391

Tennessee Department of Conservation
701 Broadway, Customs House, Nashville, TN 37219-5237
615-742-6745

Texas Parks and Wildlife Department
Parks Division
4200 Smith School Road, Austin, TX 78744
512-389-4866

Utah Department of Natural Resources
Utah Division of State Parks
1636 West North Temple, Salt Lake City, UT 84116
801-538-7362

Vermont Department of Forests, Parks and Recreation
Division of State Lands
103 South Main Street, 10 South, Waterbury, VT 05676
802-244-8711

Virginia Department of Conservation and Historic Resources
Division of State Parks
203 Governor Street, Suite 306, Richmond, VA 23219
804-786-4375

Washington State Parks and Recreation Commission
7150 Cleanwater Lane KY-11, Olympia, WA 98504-5711
206-753-5757

West Virginia Division of Parks and Recreation
Capitol Complex
Charleston, WV 25305
304-348-2764

Wisconsin Department of Natural Resources
Bureau of Parks and Recreation, Division of Resource Management
P.O. Box 7921, Madison, WI 53707
608-266-2185

Wyoming Recreation Commission
122 West 25th Street, Cheyenne, WY 82002
307-777-6690

National Parks

The U.S. Government maintains regional offices for the national parks. Address your inquiry to the National Park Service at the addresses below. Be sure to request a copy of *The National Parks Camping Guide, The National Parks Index*, and *The National Parks: Lesser-Known Areas*. Also ask for the "National Park System Map and Guide," which is a lovely map that pinpoints some of the opportunities and includes a chart of their facilities.

The national parks with camping facilities are also listed below.

If you are interested in supporting the national parks, a membership in the National Park Conservation Association helps support the parks and also provides you with additional information. Write the association at 1015 Thirty-first Street Northwest, Washington, D.C. 20007; or call 202-944-8530.

Alaska Region
(Alaska national parklands)
2525 Gambell Street, Room 107, Anchorage, AK 99503
907-271-2738

Mid-Atlantic Region
(DE, MD, PA, VA, WV)
143 South Third Street, Philadelphia, PA 19106
215-597-3678

Midwest Region
(IL, IN, IA, KS, MI, MN, MO, NE, OH, WI)
1709 Jackson Street, Omaha, NE 68102
402-221-3477

National Capital Region
(Metro D.C. and some of MD, VA, WV)
1100 Ohio Drive Southwest, Washington, D.C. 20242
202-485-9666

North Atlantic Region
(CT, ME, MA, NH, NJ, NY, RI, VT)
15 State Street, Boston, MA 02109-3572
617-565-8888

Pacific Northwest Region
(ID, OR, WA)
83 South King Street, Suite 212, Seattle, WA 98104
206-442-0170

Rocky Mountain Region
(CO, MT, ND, SD, UT, WY)
655 Parfet Street, P.O. Box 25287, Denver, CO 80225
303-969-2503

Southeast Region
(AL, FL, GA, KY, MS, NC, SC, TN)
Richard B. Russell Federal Building
75 Spring Street Southwest, Atlanta, GA 30303
404-331-5187

Southwest Region
(northeast AZ, AR, LA, NM, OK, TX)
P.O. Box 728, Santa Fe, NM 87504
505-988-6375

Western Region
(AZ, CA, HI, NV)
Golden Gate National Recreation Area
450 Golden Gate Avenue, Box 36063, San Francisco, CA 94102
415-556-0560

National Park Service Main Office
N.P.S. U.S.D.I.
P.O. Box 37127, Washington, D.C. 20013-7127
202-343-4747

Alabama

Russell Cave National Monument
Route 1, Box 175, Bridgeport, AL 35740
205-495-2672

Alaska

Aniakchak National Monument
c/o Katmat National Park and Preserve
P.O. Box 7, King Salmon, AK 99614
907-246-3305

Bering Land Bridge National Preserve
P.O. Box 220, Nome, AK 99762
907-443-2522

Cape Krusenstern National Monument
P.O. Box 1029, Kotzebue, AK 99752
907-442-3890

Denali National Park and Preserve
P.O. Box 9, McKinley Park, AK 99755
907-683-2294

Gates of the Arctic National Park and Preserve
P.O. Box 74680, Fairbanks, AK 99707
907-456-0281

Glacier Bay National Park and Preserve
Gustavus, AK 99826
907-697-2232

Katmai National Park and Preserve
P.O. Box 7, King Salmon, AK 99613
907-246-3305

Kenai Fjords National Park
P.O. Box 1727, Seward, AK 99664
907-224-3874

Klondike Gold Rush National Historical Park
P.O. Box 517, Skagway, AK 99840
907-983-2921

Arizona

Canyon de Chelly National Monument
P.O. Box 588, Chinle, AZ 86503
602-674-5436

Casa Grande National Monument
P.O. Box 518, Coolidge, AZ 85228
602-723-3172

Chiricahua National Monument
Dos Cabezas Route
Box 6500, Willcox, AZ 85643
602-824-3560

Grand Canyon National Park
P.O. Box 129, Grand Canyon, AZ 86023
602-638-7888

Navajo National Monument
H.C. 71, Box 3, Tonalea, AZ 86044-9704
602-672-2366

Organ Pipe Cactus National Monument
Route 1, Box 100, Ajo, AZ 85321
602-387-6849

Saguaro National Monument
3693 Old Spanish Trail, Tucson, AZ 85730-5699
602-298-4249

Sunset Crater National Monument
Route 3, Box 149, Flagstaff, AZ 86004
602-527-7042

Arkansas

Buffalo National River
P.O. Box 1173, Harrison, AR 72602
501-741-5443

Hot Springs National Park
P.O. Box 1860, Hot Springs, AR 71902
501-624-3383

California

Channel Islands National Park
1901 Spinnaker Drive, Ventura, CA 93001
805-644-8157

Death Valley National Monument
Death Valley, CA 92328
619-786-2331

Devils Postpile National Monument
c/o Sequoia and Kings Canyon National Parks
Three Rivers, CA 93271
714-934-2289

Golden Gate National Recreation Area
Fort Mason Building 201, San Francisco, CA 94123
415-556-0560

Joshua Tree National Monument
74485 National Monument Drive, Twenty-nine Palms, CA 92277
619-367-7511

Kings Canyon National Park
Three Rivers, CA 93271
209-565-3341

Lassen Volcanic National Park
P.O. Box 100, Mineral, CA 96063-0100
916-595-4444

Lava Beds National Monument
P.O. Box 867, Tulelake, CA 96134
916-667-2282

Muir Woods National Monument
Mill Valley, CA 94941
415-388-2595

Pinnacles National Monument
Paicines, CA 95043
408-389-4485

Point Reyes National Seashore
Point Reyes, CA 94956
415-663-8522

Redwood National Park
1111 Second Street, Crescent City, CA 95531
707-464-6101

Sequoia National Park
Three Rivers, CA 93271
209-565-3341

Whiskeytown-Shasta Whiskeytown Unit Trinity National Recreation Area
P.O. Box 188, Whiskeytown, CA 96095
916-241-6584

Yosemite National Park
P.O. Box 577, Yosemite National Park, CA 95389
209-372-0200

Colorado

Black Canyon of the Gunnison National Monument
P.O. Box 1648, Montrose, CO 81402
303-249-7036

Colorado National Monument
Fruita, CO 81521
303-858-3617

Curecanti National Recreation Area
102 Elk Creek, Gunnison, CO 81230
303-641-2337

Dinosaur National Monument
P.O. Box 210, Dinosaur, CO 81610
303-374-2216

Great Sand Dunes National Monument
Mosca, CO 81146
303-378-2312

Mesa Verde National Park
Mesa Verde National Park, CO 81330
303-529-4465

Rocky Mountain National Park
Estes Park, CO 80517
303-586-2371

Florida

Biscayne National Park
P.O. Box 1369, Homestead, FL 33090
305-247-2044

Everglades National Park
P.O. Box 279, Homestead, FL 33030
305-247-6211

Fort Jefferson National Monument
c/o Everglades National Park
P.O. Box 279, Homestead, FL 33030
305-247-6211

Gulf Islands National Seashore
1801 Gulf Breeze Parkway, Gulf Breeze, FL 32561
904-934-2613

Georgia

Chickamauga and Chattanooga National Military Park
P.O. Box 2128, Fort Oglethorpe, GA 30742
615-752-5213

Cumberland Island National Seashore
P.O. Box 806, Sait Marys, GA 31558
912-882-4337

Idaho

Craters of the Moon National Monument
P.O. Box 29, Arco, ID 83213-0029
208-527-3257

Kentucky

Cumberland Gap National Historical Park
P.O. Box 1848, Middlesboro, KY 40965-1848
606-248-2817

Mammoth Cave National Park
Mammoth Cave, KY 42259
502-758-2251

Maine

Acadia National Park
P.O. Box 177, Bar Harbor, ME 04609
207-288-9561

Maryland

Antietam National Battlefield
P.O. Box 158, Sharpsburg, MD 21782
301-432-5124

Assateague Island National Seashore
Route 2, Berlin, MD 21811
301-641-1443

Cacoctin Mountain Park
6602 Foxville Road, Thurmont, MD 21788
301-663-9343

Chesapeake and Ohio Canal National Historical Park
P.O. Box 4, Sharpsburg, MD 21782
301-739-4200

Greenbelt Park
6565 Greenbelt Road, Greenbelt, MD 20770
301-344-3948

Michigan

Isle Royale National Park
87 North Ripley Street, Houghton, MI 49931
906-482-0916

Pictured Rocks National Lakeshore
P.O. Box 40, Munising, MI 49862
906-387-2607

Sleeping Bear Dunes National Lakeshore
P.O. Box 277, 9922 Front Street, Empire, MI 49630
616-326-5134

Minnesota

Grand Portage National Monument
P.O. Box 666, Grand Marais, MN 55604
218-387-2788

Pipestone National Monument
P.O. Box 727, Pipestone, MN 56164
507-825-5464

Voyageurs National Park
P.O. Box 50, International Falls, MN 56649
218-283-9821

Mississippi

Natchez Trace Parkway
R.R. 1 NT-143, Tupelo, MS 38801
601-842-1572

Missouri

George Washington Carver National Monument
P.O. Box 38, Diamond, MO 64840
417-325-4151

Ozark National Scenic Riverways
P.O. Box 490, Van Buren, MO 63965
314-323-4236

Montana

Bighorn Canyon National Recreation Area
P.O. Box 458, Fort Smith, MT 59035
406-666-2412

Nevada

Great Basin National Park
Baker, NV 89311
702-234-7331

Lake Mead National Recreation Area
601 Nevada Highway, Boulder City, NV 89005-2426
702-293-8920

New Mexico

Bandelier National Monument
Los Alamos, NM 87544
505-672-3861

Chaco Culture National Historical Park
Star Route 4, Box 6500, Bloomfield, NM 87413
505-988-6716

El Morro National Monument
Ramah, NM 87321
505-783-4226

New York

Fire Island National Seashore
120 Laurel Street, Patchogue, NY 11772
516-289-4810

North Carolina

Blue Ridge Parkway
700 Northwestern Plaza, Asheville, NC 28801
704-259-0718

Cape Hatteras National Seashore
Route 1, Box 675, Manteo, NC 27954
919-473-2111

Cape Lookout National Seashore
P.O. Box 690, Beaufort, NC 28516
919-728-2121

North Dakota

Theodore Roosevelt National Park
P.O. Box 7, Medora, ND 58645
701-623-4466

Oklahoma

Chickasaw National Recreation Area
P.O. Box 201, Sulphur, OK 73086
405-622-3161

Oregon

Crater Lake National Park
P.O. Box 7, Crater Lake, OR 97604
503-594-2211

Pennsylvania

Delaware Water Gap National Recreation Area
Bushkill, PA 18324
717-588-2435

Fort Necessity National Battlefield
The National Pike
RD 2, Box 528, Farmington, PA 15437
412-329-5512

Gettysburg National Military Park
Gettysburg, PA 17325
717-334-1124

South Dakota

Badlands National Park
P.O. Box 6, Interior, SD 57750
605-433-5361

Wind Cave National Park
Hot Springs, SD 57747
605-745-4600

Tennessee

Big South Fork National River and Recreation Area
P.O. Drawer 630, Oneida, TN 37841
615-879-4890

Great Smoky Mountains National Park
Gatlinburg, TN 37738
615-436-1201

Texas

Amistad Recreation Area
P.O. Box 420367, Del Rio, TX 78842-0367
512-775-7491

Big Bend National Park
Big Bend National Park, TX 79834
915-477-2251

Guadalupe Mountains National Park
H.C. 60, Box 400, Salt Flat, TX 79847-9400
915-828-3251

Lake Meredith Recreation Area
P.O. Box 1438, Fritch, TX 79036
806-857-3151

Padre Island National Seashore
9405 South Padre Island Drive
Corpus Christi, TX 78418-5597

Utah

Arches National Park
P.O. Box 907, Moab, UT 84532
801-259-8161

Bryce Canyon National Park
Bryce Canyon, UT 84717
801-834-5322

Canyonlands National Park
125 West 200 South, Moab, UT 84532
801-259-7164

Capitol Reef National Park
Torrey, UT 84775
801-425-3791

Cedar Breaks National Monument
P.O. Box 749, Cedar City, UT 84720
801-586-9451

Glen Canyon National Recreation Area
P.O. Box 1507, Page, AZ 86040
602-645-2471

Hovenways National Monument
McElmo Route, Cortez, CO 81321
303-529-4465

Zion National Park
Springdale, UT 84767-1099
801-772-3256

Virginia

Prince William Forest Park
P.O. Box 209, Triangle, VA 22172
703-221-7181

Shenandoah National Park
Route 4, Box 292, Luray, VA 22835
703-999-2243

Washington

Coulee Dam National Recreation Area
P.O. Box 37, Coulee Dam, WA 99116
509-633-0881

Mount Rainier National Park
Tahoma Woods, Star Route, Ashford, WA 98304-9801
206-569-2211

North Cascades National Park Service Complex
2105 Highway 20, Sedro Woolley, WA 98284-9314
206-855-1331

Olympic National Park
600 East Park Avenue, Port Angeles, WA 98362
206-452-4501

Wisconsin

Apostle Island National Lakeshore
Route 1, Box 4, Bayfield, WI 54814
715-779-3397

Wyoming

Devils Tower National Monument
Devils Tower, WY 82714
307-467-5370

Grand Teton National Park
P.O. Box 170, Moose, WY 83012
307-733-2880

Yellowstone National Park
P.O. Box 168, Yellowstone National Park, WY 82190
307-344-7381

U.S. Forest Service

The printouts you receive when you write the U.S. Forest Service offices are very informative. You will get overview policy information and listings of the camping opportunities in your area. Be sure to ask for "A Guide to Your National Forests," a beautiful, glossy map with addresses and telephone numbers of the facilities in the nine regions. Write or call the facilities of interest to obtain more specific information.

Alaska Region (AK)
Federal Office Building
709 West Ninth Street, P.O. Box 21628, Juneau, AK 99802
907-586-8863

Eastern Region
(IL, IN, OH, MI, MN, MO, NH, ME, PA, VT, WV, WI)
310 West Wisconsin Avenue, Room 500, Milwaukee, WI 53203
414-291-3693

Intermountain Region
(ID, NV, UT, WY)
Federal Building
324 25th Street, Ogden, UT 84401
801-625-5354

Northern Region
(ID, MT)
Federal Building
200 East Broadway Street, P.O. Box 7669, Missoula, MT 59807
406-329-3511

Pacific Northwest Region
(OR, WA)
319 Southwest Pine Street, P.O. Box 3623, Portland, OR 97208
503-221-2877

Pacific Southwest Region
(CA)
630 Sansome Street, San Francisco, CA 94111
415-556-0122

Rocky Mountain Region
(CO, NE, SD WY)
11177 West Eighth Avenue, P.O. Box 25127, Lakewood, CO 80225
303-236-9431

Southern Region
(AL, AR, FL, GA, KY, LA, MS, NC, SC, TN, TX, VA)
1720 Peachtree Road Northwest, Atlanta, GA 30367
404-347-4191

Southwest Region
(AZ, NM)
Federal Building
517 Gold Avenue Southwest, Albuquerque, NM 87102
505-842-3292

U.S. Army Corps of Engineers

The Army Corps of Engineers has more than 1,500 recreation areas with camping facilities. There are ten divisions of the Army Corps; each one has a beautiful map pinpointing the recreation sites and a chart showing the facilities at the sites. You can also write a district office and request detailed information about each lake with camping facilities in the district. If you need maps of all the regions, the main office in Washington, D.C., has them.

Camping at Army Corps sites is available on a first-come-first-serve basis with no reservations.

U.S. Army Corps of Engineers Main Office
20 Massachusetts Avenue, Washington, D.C. 20314-1000
202-272-0247

LOWER MISSISSIPPI VALLEY DIVISION
P.O. Box 80, Vicksburg, MS 39180-0080
601-634-5885

St. Louis District
210 Tucker Boulevard North, St. Louis, MO 63101-1986
314-263-5533

Vicksburg District
P.O. Box 60, Vicksburg, MS 39180-0060
601-631-5300

MISSOURI RIVER DIVISION
P.O. Box 103, Downtown Station, Omaha, NE 68101-0103
402-221-7284/7285

Kansas City District
700 Federal Building, Kansas City, MO 64106-2896
816-426-5758

Omaha District
215 North 17th Street, Omaha, NE 68102-4978
402-221-4139

NEW ENGLAND DIVISION
424 Trapelo Road, Waltham, MA 02254-9149
617-647-8305

NORTH ATLANTIC DIVISION
90 Church Street, New York, NY 10007-9998
212-264-7534

Baltimore District
P.O. Box 1715, Baltimore, MD 21203-1715
301-962-3693

New York District
26 Federal Plaza, New York, NY 10278-0090
212-264-4662

Norfolk District
803 Front Street, Norfolk, VA 23510-1096
804-446-3641

Philadelphia District
U.S. Custom House
2nd and Chestnut Street, Philadelphia, PA 19106-2991
215-597-4741

NORTH CENTRAL DIVISION
536 South Clark Street, Chicago, IL 60605-1592
312-353-7762

Buffalo District
1776 Niagara Street, Buffalo, NY 14207-3199
716-876-5454 ext. 2284

Chicago District
219 South Dearborn Street, Chicago, IL 60604-1797
312-353-6432

Detroit District
P.O. Box 1027, Detroit MI 48231-1027
313-226-2256

Rock Island District
P.O. Box 2004, Clock Tower Building, Rock Island, IL 61204-20004
309-788-6361 ext. 332

St. Paul District
1421 USPO and Custom House
180 East Kellog Blvd., St. Paul, MN 55101-1429
612-220-0325

NORTH PACIFIC DIVISION
P.O. Box 2870, Portland, OR 97208-2870
503-326-4087

Alaska District
P.O. Box 898, Anchorage, AK 99506-0898
907-753-2753

Portland District
P.O. Box 2946, Portland, OR 97208-2946
503-326-6075

Seattle District
P.O. Box C-3755, Seattle, WA 98124-2255
206-764-3440

Walla Walla District
Building 602, City-County Airport, Walla Walla, WA 99362-9265
509-522-6714

OHIO RIVER DIVISION
P.O. Box 1159, Cincinnati, OH 45201-1159
513-684-3192

Huntington District
502 Eighth Street, Huntington, WV 25701-2070
304-529-5607

Louisville District
P.O. Box 59, Louisville, KY 40201-0059
502-582-5584

Nashville District
P.O. Box 1070, Nashville, TN 37202-1070
615-736-5115

Pittsburgh District
1000 Liberty Avenue, Pittsburgh, PA 15222-4186
412-644-4190

SOUTH ATLANTIC DIVISION
Room 313, 77 Forsythe St., SW, Atlanta, GA 30335-6801
404-331-6746 or -4834 or -6807

Jacksonville District
400 West Bay Street, P.O. Box 4970, Jacksonville, FL 32232-0019
904-791-2215

Mobile District
109 Saint Joseph Street, P.O. Box 2288, Mobile, AL 36628-0001
205-694-3720

Savannah District
P.O. Box 889, Savannah, GA 31402-0889
912-944-5343

Wilmington District
308 Water Street, P.O. Box 1890, Wilmington, NC 28401-1890
919-251-4827

Charleston District
P.O. Box 919, Charleston, SC 29402-0919
803-724-4677

SOUTH PACIFIC DIVISION
630 Sansome Street, Room 1216, San Francisco, CA 94111-2206
415-556-2648

Los Angeles District
P.O. Box 2711, Los Angeles, CA 90053-2325
213-894-5635

Sacramento District
650 Capitol Mall, Sacramento, CA 95814-4794
916-551-2112

San Francisco District
211 Main Street, San Francisco, CA 94105-1905
415-332-3871

SOUTHWESTERN DIVISION
1114 Commerce Street, Dallas, TX 75242-0216
214-767-2435 or -2434 or -2431

Albuquerque District
P.O. Box 1580, Albuquerque, NM 87103-1580
505-766-2724

Fort Worth District
P.O. Box 17300, Fort Worth, TX 76102-0300
817-334-2705

Galveston District
P.O. Box 1229, Galveston, TX 77553-1229
409-766-3979

Little Rock District
P.O. Box 867, Little Rock, AR 72203-0867
501-378-5673

Tulsa District
P.O. Box 61, Tulsa, OK 74121-0061
918-581-7340

U.S. Bureau of Land Management

The Bureau of Land Management manages public land in the west-ernmost states for recreational use. Most of the land is open for camping—a wonderful resource for primitive camping in wilderness areas. The regional office will send you an overview with maps pin-pointing the sites and listing their addresses and telephone numbers. The maps also include a chart designating the facilities at each site. You can write or call each site for specific information.

Write the Bureau of Land Management at one of the following addresses.

Alaska State Office
701 "C" Street, Box 13, Anchorage, AK 99513
907-271-5555

Arizona State Office
P.O. Box 16563, Phoenix, AZ 85011
602-241-5504

California State Office
2800 Cottage Way, Room E-2841, Sacramento, CA 95825
916-978-4746

Colorado State Office
2850 Youngfield Street, Lakewood, CO 80215
303-294-7090

Eastern States Office
(All other states)
350 South Pickett Street, Alexandria, VA 22304
703-274-0190

Idaho State Office
3380 Americana Terrace, Boise, ID 83706
208-334-1770

Montana State Office
(North Dakota, South Dakota)
P.O. Box 36800, Billings, MT 59107
406-657-6561

Nevada State Office
850 Harvard Way, P.O. Box 12000, Reno, NV 89520
702-784-5311

New Mexico State Office
(Oklahoma, Kansas, Texas)
Joseph M. Montoya Federal Building
P.O. Box 1449, Santa Fe, NM 87504-1449
505-988-6316

Oregon State Office
(Washington)
825 Northeast Multinomah Street, P.O. Box 2965, Portland, OR 97208
503-231-6274

Utah State Office
324 South State Street, Salt Lake City, UT 84111-2303
801-524-3146

Wyoming State Office
(Nebraska)
2515 Warren Avenue, P.O. Box 1828, Cheyenne, WY 82003
307-772-2111

The U.S. Bureau of Reclamation

The Bureau of Reclamation promotes recreation, including camping, on water sites in seventeen western states. They manage some of these sites, but the majority are operated by local, county, state, or federal agencies. Write or call the Bureau at one of the following addresses for information about their camping facilities. You may receive detailed brochures with addresses and telephone numbers of each facility.

Pacific Northwest Region
Federal Building and U.S. Courthouse
550 West Fort Street, P.O. Box 043, Boise, ID 83724
208-334-1938

Mid-Pacific Region
Federal Office Building
2800 Cottage Way, Sacramento, CA 95825-1898
916-978-4919

Lower Colorado Region
P.O. Box 427, Nevada Highway and Park Street, Boulder City, NV 89005
702-293-8419

Upper Colorado Region
125 South State Street, P.O. Box 11568, Salt Lake City, UT 84147
801-524-5403

Great Plains Region
316 North 26th Street, P.O. Box 36900, Billings, MT 59107-6900
406-657-6218

Private Agencies

There are some large private agencies operating campgrounds that
you may find of interest. Some of them are best for RV campers, and
some are good for tent camping resources. Don't overlook the hydro-
electric project sites, which are good camping areas in many states.

American Automobile Association
Campbooks, tourbooks, and maps are available at no cost to members only.
Contact your local AAA office, which is listed in telephone directory and on
your membership card.

Boy Scouts of America (registered members)
1325 Walnut Hill Lane, Irving TX 75062-1296
214-580-2000

Hydroelectric project sites
Check telephone directory under electric utility companies, municipal utilities, state-sponsored utility organizations, rural electric cooperatives, and
industrial organizations.

Kampgrounds of America (KOA)
(Send $3.00 for the "KOA Directory Road and Camping Guide")
KOA Directory, P.O. Box 30162-BL, Billings, MT 59107
406-248-7444

RV State Campgrounds Associations
Recreation Vehicle Industry Association
P.O. Box 2999, 1896 Preston White Drive, Reston, VA 22090
707-620-6033

Yogi Bear Jellystone Park Camp Resorts and Safari Campgrounds
Leisure Systems
Route 209, Bushkill, PA 18324
1-800-358-9165 (for information or a directory)
1-800-558-2954 (for reservations)

Canada

For information on camping in the Canadian provinces, write the provincial tourism offices. Be certain you mention you are looking for all possible camping-related information.

Alberta

Travel Alberta
10025 Jasper Avenue, 15th floor, Edmonton, Alberta, Canada T5J 3Z3
1-800-661-8888

British Columbia

Ministry of Tourism, Recreation and Culture
Parliament Buildings
Victoria, British Columbia, Canada V8V 1X4
1-800-663-6000

Manitoba

Travel Manitoba
Department 6020
155 Carlton Street, 7th floor, Winnipeg, Manitoba, Canada R3C 3H8
1-800-665-0040

New Brunswick

Tourism, Recreation and Heritage
Casier Postal, P.O. Box 12345, Fredericton, New Brunswick
Canada E3B 5C3
1-800-561-0123

Newfoundland-Labrador

Department of Development and Tourism
P.O. Box 2016, Station A, St. John's, Newfoundland, Canada A1C 5R8
1-800-563-6353

Nova Scotia

Department of Tourism
P.O. Box 130, Halifax, Nova Scotia, Canada B3J 2M7
1-800-341-6096

Northwest Territories

TravelArctic
Government of the Northwest Territories
Yellowknife, Northwest Territories, Canada X1A 2L9
1-800-661-0788

Ontario

Ministry of Tourism and Recreation
Queen's Park, Toronto, Ontario, Canada M7A 2E5
1-800-268-3735

Prince Edward Island

Department of Tourism and Parks
Visitor Services
P.O. Box 940, Charlottetown, Prince Edward Island, Canada, C1A 7M5
1-800-561-0123

Québec

Tourisme Québec
P.O. Box 20,000, Québec City, Québec, Canada G1K 7X2
1-800-443-7000

Saskatchewan
Tourism Saskatchewan
1919 Saskatchewan Drive, Regina, Saskatchewan, Canada S4P 3V7
1-800-667-7191

Yukon

Tourism Yukon
P.O. Box 2703, Whitehorse, Yukon, Canada Y1A 2C6
403-667-5340

CAMPING-RELATED INFORMATION

U.S. Fish and Wildlife Services

The Fish and Wildlife Service has a lovely , glossy map, "National Wildlife Refuges: A Visitor's Guide." The colorful chart on the back of the map lists the specific activities offered at every site in the United States with visitor opportunities. There are a few with camping, but more common are recreation activities such as trails, boating, bicycling, hunting, fishing, and a visitor's station. The map gives addresses for the sites' managing offices so you can write them for detailed information.

U.S. Fish and Wildlife Service
Washington, D.C. 20240
202-343-4311

Region I (CA, ID, HI, NV, OR, WA)
Lloyd 500 Building
Suite 1692, 500 Northeast Multinomah Street, Portland, OR 97232
503-231-6118

Region II (AZ, NM, OK, TX)
Box 1306, Albuquerque, NM 87103
505-766-2321

Region III (IL, IN, IA, MI, MN, MO, OH, WI)
Federal Building, Fort Snelling, Twin Cities, MN 55111
612-725-3563

Region IV (AR, AL, FL, GA, KY, LA, MS, NC, SC, TN, PR)
75 Spring Street Southwest, Atlanta, GA 30303
404-331-3588

Region V (CT, DE, MA, MD, ME, NH, NJ, PA, VA, VT, WV)
One Gateway Center, Suite 700, Newton Corner, MA 02158
617-965-5100

Region VI (CO, KS, MT, NE, ND, SD, UT, WY)
Box 25486, Denver Federal Center, Denver, CO 80225
303-236-7920

Region VII (AK)
1011 East Tudor Road, Anchorage, AK 99503
907-786-3542

State Offices of Tourism

Don't miss this resource. By writing a state office of tourism, you will get a large packet of materials that usually includes a colorful booklet with recreation opportunities, map, folders, and local attractions. Say that you are especially interested in their camping information (otherwise, they might not send it in order to keep their postage costs at a minimum). A number of states print a directory specifically about camping opportunities in the state, and others include a comprehensive section on camping in their state tourism guide.

Alabama Bureau of Tourism and Travel
532 South Perry Street, Montgomery, AL 36104
1-800-392-8096 (in state)
1-800-ALABAMA (out of state)

Alaska Division of Tourism
P.O. Box E-301, Juneau, AK 99811-0800
907-465-2010

Arizona Office of Tourism
1100 West Washington, Phoenix, AZ 85007
1-800-221-5596 (in state)
1-800-528-0483 (out of state)

Arkansas Department of Parks and Tourism
1 Capitol Mall, Little Rock, AR 72201
1-800-482-8999 (in state)
1-800-643-8383 (out of state)

California Department of Tourism
Visitor Information Center
1121 L Street, Suite 600, Sacramento, CA 95814
1-800-862-2543 (in state)
1-800-TO-CALIF (out of state)

Colorado Tourism Board
1625 Broadway, Suite 1700, Denver, CO 80202
1-800-433-2656

Connecticut Department of Economic Development
210 Washington Street, Hartford, CT 06106
1-800-842-7492 (in state)
1-800-243-1685 (northeastern USA)

Delaware Tourism Office
99 Kings Highway, Box 1401, Dover, DE 19903-9904
1-800-282-8667 (in state)
1-800-441-8846 (out of state)

Florida Department of Commerce
Division of Tourism
Visitor Inquiry
1266 Van Buren Street, Tallahassee, FL 32399-2000
904-487-1462

Georgia Department of Industry and Trade
P.O. Box 1776, Atlanta, GA 30301
404-656-3590

Hawaii Visitors Bureau
1511 K Street Northwest, Suite 415, Washington, D.C. 20005
202-393-6752

Idaho Travel Council
State Capitol Building
700 West State Street, Boise, ID 83720
1-800-635-7820

Illinois Office of Tourism
Department of Commerce and Community Affairs
310 South Michigan Avenue, Suite 108, Chicago, IL 60604
312-793-2094
1-800-223-0121 (out of state)

Indiana Department of Commerce
Tourism Development Division
1 North Capitol Avenue, Suite 700, Indianapolis, IN 46204-2288
1800-2-WANDER

Iowa Tourism Bureau
Division of Economic Development
200 East Grand, Des Moines, IA 50309
1-800-345-IOWA

Kansas Travel and Tourism
400 West Eighth Street, 5th Floor, Topeka, KS 66603-3957
913-296-2009 1-800-2-KANSAS (in state)

Kentucky Department of Travel Development
Capitol Plaza Tower
Frankfort, KY 40601
1-800-225-TRIP

Louisiana Department of Culture, Recreation and Tourism
Office of Tourism
P.O. Box 94291, Baton Rouge, LA 70804-9291
504-925-3860
1-800-231-4730 (out of state)

Maine Tourism Information Services
The Maine Publicity Bureau, Inc.
97 Winthrop Street, P.O. Box 2300, Hallowell, ME 04347-2300
207-289-2423

Maryland Office of Tourist Development
45 Calvert Street, Annapolis, MD 21401
1-800-331-1750

Massachusetts Division of Tourism
100 Cambridge Street, 13th Floor, Boston, MA 02202
1-800-858-0200

Michigan Department of Commerce
Travel Bureau
P.O. Box 30226, Lansing, MI 48909
1-800-5432-YES

Minnesota Office of Tourism
375 Jackson Street, 250 Skyway Level, St. Paul, MN 55101-1810
1-800-652-9747 (in state)
1-800-328-1461 (out of state)

Mississippi Department of Economic Development
Division of Tourism

P.O. Box 849, Jackson, MS 39205
1-800-647-2290

Missouri Division of Tourism
301 West High Street, Truman Building
P.O. Box 1055, Jefferson City, MO 65102
314-751-4133

Montana Travel Promotion Division
1424 Ninth Avenue, Helena, MT 59620
406-444-2654
1-800-541-1447 (out of state)

Nebraska Department of Economic Development
Division of Travel and Tourism
301 Centennial Mall South, P.O. Box 94666, Lincoln, NE 68509-4666
1-800-742-7595 (in state)
1-800-228-4307 (out of state)

Nevada Commission on Tourism
Capitol Complex
Carson City, NV 89710
702-885-4322
1-800-638-2328 (out of state)

New Hampshire Office of Vacation Travel
P.O. Box 856, Concord, NH 03301
603-271-2666

New Jersey Division of Travel and Tourism
CN826
Trenton, NJ 08625-0826
609-292-2470

New Mexico Travel Division
Joseph Montoya Building
1100 Saint Francis Drive, P.O. Box 20003, Santa Fe, NM 87504
505-827-0291
1-800-545-2040 (out of state)

New York State Department of Economic Development
One Commerce Plaza, Albany, NY 12245
518-474-4116
1-800-CALL-NYS (out of state)

North Carolina Department of Commerce
Division of Travel and Tourism
430 North Salisbury Street, Raleigh, NC 27611
919-733-4171
1-800-VISIT-NC (out of state)

North Dakota Tourism Promotion
Liberty Memorial Building
State Capitol Grounds, Bismarck, ND 58505
1-800-472-2100 (in state)
1-800-437-2077 (out of state)
1-800-537-8879 (Canada)

Ohio Department of Development
P.O. Box 1001, Columbus, OH 43216
1-800-BUCK-EYE

Oklahoma Tourism and Recreation Department
Literature Distribution Center
P.O. Box 60000, Oklahoma City, OK 73146
1-800-652-6552

Oregon Economic Development Department
Tourism Division
595 Cottage Street Northeast, Salem, OR 97301
1-800-543-8838 (in state)
1-800-547-7842 (out of state)

Pennsylvania Department of Commerce
Division of Travel Marketing
230 South Broad Street, 5th Floor, Philadelphia, PA 19102-3816
1-800-VISIT-PA

Rhode Island Department of Economic Development
7 Jackson Walkway, Providence, RI 02903
401-277-2601
1-800-556-2484 (from ME to VA, also WV and OH)

South Carolina Division of Tourism
P.O. Box 71, Columbia, SC 29202-0071
803-253-6319

South Dakota Tourism
Capitol Lake Plaza, Pierre, SD 57501
1-800-952-2217 (in state)
1-800-843-1930 (out of state)

Tennessee Tourism Development
P.O. Box 23170, Nashville, TN 37202-3170
615-741-2158

Texas Department of Highways and Public Transportation
Travel and Information Division
P.O. Box 5064, Austin, TX 78763-5064
512-465-7401

Utah Travel Council
Council Hall/Capitol Hill
Salt Lake City, UT 84114
1-800-533-5681

Vermont Travel Division
Agency of Development and Community Affairs
134 State Street, Montpelier, VT 05602
802-828-3236

Virginia Division of Tourism
202 North Ninth Street, Suite 500, Richmond, VA 23219
804-786-4484

Washington Department of Trade and Economic Development
General Administration Building
Olympia, WA 98504-0613
1-800-562-4570 (in state)
1-800-541-9274 (out of state)

West Virginia Department of Commerce
Tourism Division
1900 Washington Street East
Building 6, Charleston, WV 25305
1-800-CALL-WVA

Wisconsin Department of Development
Division of Tourism
P.O. Box 7606, Madison, WI 53707
608-266-2161

Wyoming Travel Commission
Frank Norris, Jr. Travel Center
I-25 College Avenue, Cheyenne, WY 82002
307-777-7777
1-800-CALL-WYO (out of state)

Lake-Map Information for Fishing

Some states provide fishing information upon request. You may receive a packet of information containing pamphlets on fishing seasons and regulations, a guide to lakes and reservoirs and specialty-local fishing, maps, and more. In addition the U.S. Geological Survey offices have maps that tell fishermen what they need to know about the depth of different lakes. If you send them specific questions about underwater conditions, they will research and answer them.

Arkansas Game and Fish Commission
2 Natural Resources Drive, Little Rock, AR 72205
501-223-6300

California Department of Fish and Game
Conservation Education
1416 Ninth Street, 12th Floor, Sacramento, CA 95814
916-445-7613

Connecticut Natural Resource Center
Publication Sales, Room 555, 165 Capitol Avenue, Hartford CT 06106
203-566-7719

Delaware Department of Natural Resources and Environmental Control
Division of Fish and Wildlife
P.O. Box 1401, 89 Kings Highway, Dover, DE 19903
302-736-3441

Georgia Department of Natural Resources
Maps and Publications
19 Martin Luther King Jr. Drive Southwest, Room 406A, 4th Floor
Atlanta, GA 30334
404-656-3214

Idaho Department of Fish and Game
600 South Walnut, Box 25, Boise, ID 83707
208-334-3700

Illinois Department of Conservation
Division of Fisheries
Lincoln Tower Plaza, 524 South Second Street
Springfield, IL 62701-1787
217-782-6424

Indiana Department of Natural Resources
Map Sales Section
612 State Office Building, Indianapolis, IN 46204
317-232-4180

Kansas Department of Wildlife and Parks
Fish and Game Commission
Route 2, Box 54A, Pratt, KS 67124-9599
316-672-5911

Kentucky Department of Economic Development
Maps and Publications
133 Holmes Street, Frankfort, KY 40601
502-564-4715

Louisiana Department of Wildlife and Fisheries
Fish Division
P.O. Box 98000, Baton Rouge, LA 70898-9000
504-765-2360

Maryland Department of Natural Resources
Tidewater Administration - Fisheries
Tawes State Office Building, C-2
580 Taylor Avenue, Annapolis, MD 21401
301-974-3764

Massachusetts Division of Fisheries and Wildlife
Field Headquarters
Westboro, MA 01581
508-366-4479

Mississippi Department of Natural Resources
Bureau of Geology
P.O. Box 5348, Jackson, MS 39216
601-354-6228

Missouri Department of Conservation
P.O. Box 180, Jefferson City, MO 65102-0180
314-751-4115

Montana Department of Fish, Wildlife, and Parks
1420 East Sixth Avenue, Helena, MT 59620
406-444-2449

Nebraska Game and Parks Commission
P.O. Box 30370, Lincoln, NE 68503
402-471-0641

Nevada Department of Wildlife
P.O. Box 10678, Reno, NV 89520-0022
702-789-0500

New Hampshire Fish and Game Department
2 Hasen Drive, Concord, NH 03301
603-271-2501

New Jersey Division of Fish, Game and Wildlife
Wildlife Education Unit
Bureau of Freshwater Fisheries
Pequest Road, R.R. 1, Box 389, Oxford, NJ 07863
201-637-4125

New Mexico Department of Game and Fish
Villagra Building
State Capitol
Santa Fe, NM 87503
505-827-7911

New York State Department of Environmental Conservation
50 Wolf Road, Albany, NY 12233-4750
518-474-2121

Ohio Department of Natural Resources
Division of Wildlife
Fountain Square
Columbus, OH 43224
614-265-6565

Oklahoma Department of Wildlife Conservation
1801 North Lincoln, P.O. Box 53465, Oklahoma City, OK 73152
405-521-3851

Pennsylvania Fish Commission
P.O. Box 1673, Harrisburg, PA 17105-1673
717-657-4518

South Carolina Wildlife and Marine Resources Department
P.O. Box 167, Columbia, SC 29202
803-734-3888

South Dakota Department of Game, Fish and Parks
Division of Wildlife
Sigurd Anderson Building
445 East Capitol, Pierre, SD 57501-3185
605-773-3381

Tennessee Valley Authority
Mapping Services Branch
200 Haney Building, Chattanooga, TN 37401
615-751-MAPS

Texas Parks and Wildlife Department
4220 Smith School Road, Austin, TX 78744
512-389-4800

Vermont Agency of Environmental Conservation
Fish and Wildlife Department
103 South Main Street, 10 South, Waterbury, VT 05676
802-244-7331

Virginia Department of Game and Inland Fisheries
P.O. Box 11104, Richmond, VA 23230-1104
804-367-1000

West Virginia Department of Natural Resources
Wildlife Resources Division
1800 Washington Street East, Charleston, WV 25305
304-348-2771

Wyoming Game and Fish Department
5400 Bishop Boulevard, Cheyenne, WY 82002
307-777-7735

National Cartographic Information Center (NCIC)
U.S. Geological Survey
507 National Center, Reston, VA 22092
703-860-6045

U.S. Geological Survey
11400 Independence Road, Rolla, MO 65401
314-341-0851

U.S. Geological Survey
345 Middlefield Road, Menlo Park, CA 94025
415-329-4309

U.S. Geological Survey
Building 3101, Stennis Space Center, MS 39529
601-688-3544

Alaska-NCIC
U.S. Geological Survey
4230 Univsersity Drive, Anchorage, AK 99508-4664
907-271-4159

U.S. Geological Survey
Box 25046, DFC, STOP 504, Denver, CO 80225
303-236-5829

EROS Data Center
U.S. Geological Survey
Sioux Falls, SD 57198
605-594-6151

Catalogs for Camping Supplies

Catalogs are for information as well as shopping. Don't miss these resources as a way to educate yourself about the current market, prices, and terminology. Some of the following catalogs carry a variety of items related to camping; others are more specialized, as noted.

Best Products Mailing List
P.O. Box 26527, Richmond, VA 23261
1-800-221-BEST

Camping World (RV supplies)
Beech Bend Road, P.O. Box CW, Bowling Green, KY 42102-4920
1-800-633-5251 (in state)
1-800-626-5944 (out of state)

217

Campmor
P.O. Box 998, Paramus, NJ 07653
1-800-526-4784

Gander Mountain, Inc. (fishing and hunting supplies)
Box 248, Wilmot, WI 53192
1-800-558-9410

L.L. Bean, Inc.
Casco Street, Freeport, ME 04033
1-800-221-4221

The Nature Company (nature recreation items)
P.O. Box 2310, Berkeley, CA 94702
1-800-227-1114

Orienteering Services U.S.A. (orienteering materials)
Box 1604, Binghamton, NY 13902
607-724-0411

Penneys
1-800-222-6161

Recreational Equipment, Inc. (REI)
P.O. Box 88125-BL, Seattle, WA 98138-0125
1-800-426-4840

Sears
1-800-732-7786

Service Merchandise
P.O. Box 25130, Nashville, TN 37202
1-800-251-1212

The Sierra Trading Post (camp clothing)
1625 Crane Way, Sparks, NV 89431
702-355-3355

Index

About the Author

Beverly Liston is a free-lance writer from California's Silicon Valley. She has camped with her family for twenty-eight years; and with each trip she has learned more of the secrets for an enjoyable camping trip, from what gear is most important to which camping recipes are the finest.

Beverly, her husband, and two of their six children continue to camp, preferring to combine bicycling, hiking, swimming, an inflatable boat, and photography with their campsite routine.